Lunt

14917

PUBLIC LIBRARY
COLORADO SPRINGS

Fourteen Days Book
Fine for Overtime, 2 cents per day

DATE TAKEN	DATE TAKEN
JAN 2 18	
FEB 18 77	
FEB 23 45	
JAN 10 90	
NOV 3 02	
JUL 3 56	
FEB 23 36	
DEC 19 83	
MAR 3 61	
DEC 12 03 1 mo	
MAR 16 24	
JAN 11	
JUL 11 85	
APR 10	
DEC 20 65	

You Gentiles

By Maurice Samuel
Author of "The Outsider," "Whatever Gods."

New York
Harcourt, Brace and Company

Contents

You Gentiles

I

The Question

I

THESE last ten years and more I have been asking myself, with increasing urgency, a number of questions:

Is there any special significance in the distinction I have so long cherished—the distinction of "Jew-gentile"—not to be found in the class of distinctions implied in "American-Foreigner" or "Englishman-Foreigner"? Is there, between us Jews and you gentiles, that is between the Jew on the one hand and the Englishman, the Frenchman, the American on the other hand, that which transcends all the differences which exist among yourselves, so that, in relation to us, you are gentiles first, and afterwards (and without particular relevance in this connection) Englishmen, Frenchmen, Americans?

You Gentiles

Or is there nothing more implied in that distinction, Jew-gentile, than (in a general way) in the distinctions Jew-American, American-Englishman, Englishman-Frenchman?

In other words, are we Jews but part of the gentiles, Americans, Englishmen, Jews, Frenchmen, or is there a deeper cleavage between us? Is this Western world divided primarily into two parts—you gentiles; we Jews?

From the outset I shall be asked: "Even if you suspect the existence of such a primal cleavage, beyond the reach of ordinary national or racial classifications, what purpose can you have in urging it upon the attention of the world? Has it any practical application? Does it in any fashion clarify the status of the Jew, or give greater cogency to such claims of his as are still unsatisfied?"

This question will be asked of me by many Jews—but in particular it will be asked with the utmost insistence by those Jews who have based our case for national rights, national

8

equality, precisely on this assumption—that we Jews are a people like all other peoples, similar in needs and impulses: that we are Jews, you are Englishmen, you are Italians, you are Americans; that we, the world's races or peoples, are all of us similar in our differences.

Leaving on one side those who deny the existence of any distinctions at all, those, that is, who say that the Jew is either a Frenchman, an American or an Englishman according to the place of his birth, I would answer: "For me the ordinary nationalist or racial classification has not sufficed."

If I have long pondered this question of Jew and gentile it is because I suspected from the first dawning of Jewish self-consciousness that Jew and gentile are two worlds, that between you gentiles and us Jews there lies an unbridgeable gulf. Side by side with this belief grew another, which is related to the practical aspect of the distinction.

I do not believe that, situated as we are

9

in your midst, scattered among you from one end of the Western world to the other, we have the right to retain our identity if we are but another addition to the gentile peoples. (Nor, by the way, do I believe that we could have retained it so long had this been the case.) If we are but one more people added to the long roster of peoples, living and dead, we have no claim worth while, under these circumstances, to continuity of separate consciousness. Such a claim could never have arisen had we remained secure, segregated on our own soil—it would have been our tacit birthright. But as it is, our existence is secured at an infinite expense of special effort on our part, and of peculiar discomfort to you. Wherever the Jew is found he is a problem, a source of unhappiness to himself and to those around him. Ever since he has been scattered in your midst he has had to maintain a continuous struggle for the conservation of his identity. Is it worth while, in the face of this double burden, our own and yours, to perpetuate what may be, after all, an addition of one unit to scores of similar units? Were these centuries of alternate torture and respite not a disproportionately high price for the right to increase by one page the already overburdened records of the nations?

Were it my belief, as it is, at least in expression, the belief of many fellow-Jews, that our right to exist is founded on our similarity to other peoples, that where American or Belgian or Italian has a right to homeland, culture, history, parliament, we Jews have the same right, for the same reasons, and for no other reasons—were this my belief, I could not find the heart to continue the struggle or to urge the struggle upon others. The effort is too severe; the price is too high: the guerdon is insignificant. Were we like other peoples we ought to have done what other peoples, under similar circumstances, would do: a people driven from its homeland, a people ground into dust and carried by winds of misfortune into every corner of the world, has no right to inflict its woes and longings on others. It should cease to exist, it should rid the world of its importunate presence.

Such would be my belief if I saw in ourselves only the replica, with the proper variations, of the rest of the world. But this is not my belief, for I see otherwise. Years of observation and thought have given increasing strength to the belief that we Jews stand apart from you gentiles, that a primal duality breaks the humanity I know into two distinct parts; that this duality is a fundamental, and that all differences among you gentiles are trivialities compared with that which divides all of you from us.

I am aware that this is a thesis which cannot be supported by diagrams, tables and logarithms. It cannot even be urged with the apparent half-compulsion of social and economic laws. The cogency of what I have to say does not depend on reference to obvious and ineluctable laws, natural processes acknowledged and accepted. I am also aware that the weight of what is called learned opinion will be thrown against me, that my contention will meet with the ridicule of facile common sense and of scholarship. Nevertheless I set it down clearly that in this Western world there are essentially two peoples as spiritual forces, only two human sections with essential meaning—Jew and gentile.

But at least what credentials have I to offer—since the presentation of credentials must always precede the presentation of the thesis? What claim have I on the attention of the world? I can only answer that this book, being a serious book, must carry its own credentials, and does not attempt to borrow importance from outside sources. I offer myself only as a Jew who has lived, observed and thought: my experiences and contacts have been somewhat more varied than those of most men, but this has little to do with my views. The truth which is spread over the whole world is also contained in any part of it. The laws of gravitation are implied as completely in the falling of a pebble to earth as in the rush of the sun against the counter-rush of its companion stars. The law of Einstein works no less truly in the crawling of a snail than in the dizzy vibration of the fastest atomic sub-unit. These laws are more easily observed in the one set of cases than in the other: that is all.

If I have touched the truth it has been primarily through contact with life—and I have regarded books as but a class of living things, to be observed and interpreted and placed in their setting. Life itself, observation of men and women, singly and in masses, a knowledge of their works (among which books are important), a feeling for their desires, perception of their intent in cities, laws, theaters, games, wars, all this has brought me to the conception I shall set forth. All scholarship—particularly that scholarship which deals with the manifestations of man's desires and fears—consists of unauthoritative marginal notes, which are of interest chiefly as giving us some insight into the nature of those who jotted them down.

It does no harm to know the history that

14

is in books; but the only authentic history is around us. It is made daily in newspapers, theaters, meetings, election campaigns. And is it less valuable to know what the waiter said at the Simplicissimus cabaret in Vienna when I was there three years ago than to know what Terence reports a slave to have said in Rome when he was there two thousand years ago? What if my neighbor, the Professor, reads Greek rather less fluently than did a certain thick-witted Athenian citizen who lived in the time of Pericles and by no means as well as I read English? Is that proof of wisdom or understanding? And supposing my neighbor on the other side, the famous professor of History, knows rather less about the Peloponnesian war than the intelligent college student knows about the World War—is that Professor therefore wiser than most men, is his opinion on life more valuable? And supposing another scholar purports to tell us what the ancient Egyptians believed, and from his account of this dead religion pretends to teach the secrets

15

of faith. Can he tell me what John Doe or Isaac Levy believes? Does John Doe believe that Christ rose from the dead? *Really* believe that, as a plain truth, as he would believe it if his mother, whom he buried five years ago, should suddenly come walking into his house, rotted away and clad in her tattered cerements—believe it as simply and as terribly? And does Isaac Levy believe that the waters of the Red Sea were divided, as he would believe it if oné day, below the Williamsburg Bridge, he were to see the waters split, rear, and fall again? And if neither John Doe nor Isaac Levy believes as cogently as this, then what do they really believe, if they believe anything at all? And if the professor cannot answer these questions, what does he mean when he says that the Egyptians believed that Osiris rose from the dead? And what do his reports matter?

There is no test or guarantee of a man's wisdom or of his reliability beyond what he says about life itself. Life is the touchstone: books must be read and understood in order that we may compare our experience in life with the sincere report of the experience of others. But such and such a one, who has read all the books extant on history and art, is of no consequence unless these are to him an indirect commentary on what he feels around him.

Hence, if I have drawn chiefly on experience and contemplation and little on books—which others will discover without my admission—this does not affect my competency, which must be judged by standards infinitely more difficult of application. Life is not so simple that you can test a man's nearness to truth by giving him a college examination. Such examinations are mere games—they have no relation to reality. You may desire some such easy standard by which you can judge whether or not a man is reliable: Does he know much history? Much biology? Much psychology? If not, he is not worth listening to. But it is part of the frivolity of our outlook to reduce life to a set of rules, and thus save ourselves the agony of constant reference to first principles. No: standardized knowledge is no guarantee of truth. Put down a simple question—a living question, like this: "Should A. have killed B.?" Ask it of ten fools: five will say "Yes," five will say "No." Ask it of ten intelligent men: five will say "Yes," five will say "No." Ask it of ten scholars: five will say "Yes," five will say "No." The fools will have no reasons for their decision: the intelligent men will have a few reasons for and as many against; the scholars will have more reasons for and against. But where does the truth lie?

What, then, shall be the criterion of a man's reliability?

There is none. You cannot evade your responsibility thus by entrusting your salvation into the hands of a priest-specialist. A simpleton may bring you salvation and a great philosopher may confound you.

And so to life direct, as I have seen it working in others and felt it within myself, I refer the truth of what I say. And to books I refer only in so far as they are manifestations of life.

II

But another question, more subtle and disturbing, must be faced. I have said, "There are two life-forces in the world I know: Jewish and gentile, ours and yours." If this be a truth, we must not be driven from it if, like many other truths, it is overlaid and obscured by the irrelevancies of life, by the intersection and confusion of currents. Here is the gentile life-force: here is the Jewish life-force. What their origin was I cannot say. I can only surmise dimly what circumstances, reacting upon what original impulses, produced the Jewish life-force and the gentile life-force. I can only affirm—to the Jews, in the main, belongs the Jewish life-force, a consistent and coherent force, a direction in human thought and reaction. To you others belongs the gentile life-force, a mode of life and thought distinct from ours. But the border line is not clear. Not all of us Jews are representative of the Jewish life-force: not all of you gentiles are altogether alien to it.

We have lived for many centuries in close contiguity, if not in intimacy. Our prophetic books, our most characteristic influence, have been read to you for many hundreds of years. Something in these books has developed here and there, among you, a latent individual impulse to our Jewish way of life and thought. Essentially our prophetic books cannot change your gentile nature: but in stray, predestined hearts they bring forth fruit. Your outlook on life, your dominant reactions, are the same to-day as they were two thousand years ago. All that has changed is the instrument of expression. You live the same life under different faiths. But something clings to you here and there resembling the original form of the faith we gave you. Here and there our somber earnestness breaks out on the dazzling kaleidoscope of your history.

And we, for all our segregation have caught,

particularly of late, something of your way of life. As a few gentiles have spoken in Jewish tones, so more than one Jew speaks the language of the gentile. Jews live a gentile life here and there, while gentile lives give expression to Jewish emotions.

Yet the cleavage is there, abysmal and undeniable. In the main, we are forever distinct. Ours is one life, yours is another. Such accidental confusions as make some Northerners darker than Southerners does not affect the law that the Southerner is darker-skinned. The law holds none the less for accidental and contradictory cases.

You may even have Jews in your midst who did not learn their way of life from us, and did not inherit it from a Jewish forbear. We may have authentic gentiles in our midst: these single protests are of no account: they are extreme and irrelevant variations.

And of as little account are the occasional transferences of customs and conventions, taken over in the mass. We may have customs and conventions of yours imposed on

21

our fundamental way of life—even as you have the surface credo of a Jewish faith imposed on your way of life. But in the end your true nature works itself into the pattern of the borrowed faith, and expresses itself undeniably. So we, borrowing from you, finally assimilate the loan and in time make it essentially ours.

Beyond all these irrelevancies which hide at times but do not change the issue lies that clear and fateful division of life—Jewish and gentile. Because I have mingled intimately with the Jewish world and with the gentile world, I know well how easily exceptions obscure the rule: but I know just as well the unsounded abyss between us. What I have learned in your midst stands in my mind sharply severed from what I have learned in the midst of my people. I listen to your life, to the brilliant chorus which goes up from lands, governments, cities, books, churches, moralities: and in my mind I can no more confuse it with the tone of Jewish life than I could confuse the roaring of a tempest with

The Question

the deliberate utterance of the still, small voice. I repeat: it is of life I speak, of masses of men and women: of the things they say and do: of their daily selves, as I have known them. It is of life at first hand that I speak: of yourselves as you are in masses and singly, of my own people as I know them. My conviction came first from this contact, and from meditation on its meaning. I learned this belief of mine not in books, not in history, but in Manchester, Paris, Berlin, Vienna, New York. So gentiles, I concluded, have a way of living and thinking, wherever they may be. So Jews have a way of living and thinking. Had no books ever been written, were there no histories to refer to, I would have come to this belief.

I do not believe that this primal difference between gentile and Jew is reconciliable. You and we may come to an understanding, never to a reconciliation. There will be irritation between us as long as we are in intimate contact. For nature and constitution and vision divide us from all of you forever

—not a mere conviction, not a mere language, not a mere difference of national or religious allegiance. With the best will on both sides, successful adaptation to each other will always be insecure and transient. Waves of liberality may affect our mutual relationship from time to time: we shall delude ourselves—you and we—with the belief that we have bridged the gulf. Many will pass their lives in that delusion. But, as has come to pass so often, the difference which is deeper than will, deeper than consciousness, will assert itself. There is a limit to our moral or mental possibilities. We cannot climb out of ourselves. The complete and permanent reconciliation of your way of life with ours is beyond that limit.

Of course it is the frequent theme of editors, of popular professional optimists and of gullible and facile publicists that the path to reconciliation between Jew and gentile is the path of knowledge—or, rather, of information. The more you know concerning our history, our customs, our beliefs, the nearer

you will find us to you, the less you will dislike us. But this is futile (and unreliable)
amiability. It is by no means even a general
rule that the best-informed people are the
least accessible to anti-Semitism, that the
most backward countries are the most in-
fected. Here is a cult, or at least a feeling,
which sits with equal grace on the grossest
of your peasantry and the most refined of
your aristocracy. In the one case it is forti-
fied by superstition, in the other case by all
the information that "scientific" research into
philosophy, history, ethnography and anthro-
pology can accumulate. Not that, in my
opinion, the aristocrat knows us better than
the peasant, the scholar better than the boor.
But even if you should understand us—and
I offer you this toward that end—we would
not find mutual tolerance any easier.

This book, therefore, cannot be presented
as an effort to achieve an end which from
the outset is declared impossible. I do not
propose to combat anti-Semitism. I only
wish to present what seems to me its true

explanation in the hope of changing some of its manifestations.

III

We shall not come to understand the nature of the primal difference between gentile and Jew if we attempt to treat it merely as a difference in accepted dogmas and philosophies. A religion, in its formulated essence, is seldom the real religion, the practice and belief. Creeds which in their formulated essence are alien to a people may be accepted by the people. But the true nature of the people asserts itself. The form and dogma of the religion are retained: but the fabric, the institutions, the true reactions which make the religion what *it is* outside of its sacred books—these are the indices to its actual force and significance. There is such a thing as conversion of a man's opinions: there is no such thing (outside the field of long and laborious psychotherapy in individual cases) as conversion of a man's nature.

26

The Question

That is beyond the reach of conscious effort, certainly beyond the reach of the missionary. Change a man's opinions and his nature will soon learn to express itself through the new medium.

This I preface to my observations on the difference between Jew and gentile because I anticipate the commonplace allusion to the similarity of our creeds, to the identity of source and to the origin of the founder of your religion. Christianity (the reality, not the credo) is not a variant of Judaism, whatever Christ or his chroniclers may have intended. Your nature is the same to-day as it was before the advent of Christianity. Within the framework of another creed your instincts would have woven a similar design.

And if not religious, this difference certainly cannot be in the nature of a philosophy or a *Weltanschauung*. It is true that a man's nature dictates his philosophy and *Weltanschauung*, even as it does his religion. But we must also remember that our logic is nearly always at variance with our natures:

a man's nature expresses itself only indirectly —is never found in the face value of his assertions. Surely we differ in religion and philosophy—but only if we consider religion and philosophy not as assertions but as the practice, or art of life, presented in their name. Though you and we were to agree on all fundamental principles, as openly stated, though we should agree that there is only one God, that war is evil, that universal peace is the most desirable of human ideals, yet we should remain fundamentally different. The language of our external expression is alike, but the language of our internal meaning is different. You call that line, in that part of the spectrum, red; so do we. But who will ever know that the sensation "red" in you is the sensation "red" in us?

Life is fluid and dogmas are fixed: and life, trying to come to terms with dogmas, does not easily break with them, but endows them with almost infinite plasticity. Under the same dogmas a man will kill another or die rather than lift his hand to kill. One generation means one thing in a dogma: another generation means another thing. And at last even the elasticity of the dogma will not stand the strain: a sudden wave of emotion comes to reinforce accumulated resentment: there is a revolution and a new religion is founded; new dogmas are accepted. Perhaps they do not answer the need; perhaps they express only a passing fashion; perhaps they are no nearer than the old dogmas to a reconciliation between philosophy and instinct. But they may take root. And the process begins all over again. Instinct endures for glacial ages; religions revolve with civilizations.

Let us differentiate, then, between a religion as a dogma and the same religion as a practised art or way of life. We may compare religion with religion: that is legitimate and fruitful. But let us, in so doing, compare dogma with dogma, practice with practice: and even when we treat of dogma let us be careful to distinguish between the dogma as proclaimed and the dogma as it is transmuted by the emotions.

29

You Gentiles

And certainly between the dogmas of your religions and ours there is little difference— for we gave you the dogmas. It is absurd to assert that the sole difference between you and us is that you believe the Messiah has already come while we believe that he is yet to come; or that you believe (even in theory) in the doctrine of forgiveness while we believe in the doctrine of retaliation. Even in theory this difference is trifling in the face of the overwhelming bulk of common inspiration. The difference between us is abysmal: it is not a disagreement about a historic fact or about a commandment which neither of us observes. In some of these dogmatic disagreements we may find the key to our differences: they do not constitute the difference. A few of them (those which have not been stretched to accommodate your instincts but express them readily) were caused by the difference between us. They did not cause it.

That primal difference, which I have sensed more and more keenly as I have tasted more and more of life, your life and our life,

The Question

is a difference in the sum totals of our re-
spective emotions under the stimulus of the
external world; it is a difference in the essential quality or tone of our mental and
spiritual being. Life is to you one thing—
to us another. And according to these two
essential qualities we make answer to the
needs and impulses which are common to
both of us.

To you life is a game and a gallant adventure, and all life's enterprises partake of
the spirit of the adventurous. To us life is
a serious and sober duty pointed to a definite
and inescapable task. Your relations to gods
and men spring from the joy and rhythm of
the temporary comradeship or enmity of
spirit. Our relation to God and men is dic-
tated by a somber subjection to some eternal
principle. Your way of life, your moralities
and codes, are the rules of a game—none the
less severe or exacting for that, but not inspired by a sense of fundamental purposeful-
ness. Our way of life, our morality and code,
do not refer to temporary rules which govern

a temporary and trivial pastime: they are inspired by a belief (a true belief, a belief
which reaches below assertion into instinctive
reaction) in the eternal quality of human en-
deavor. To you morality is "the right
thing," to us morality is "right." For all the
changing problems of human relationship
which rise with changing circumstances you
lay down the rules and regulations of the
warrior, the sportsman, the gentleman; we
refer all problems seriously to eternal law.
For you certain acts are "unbecoming" to
the pertinent ideal type—whether he be a
knight or a "decent fellow." We have no
such changing systems of reference—only one
command.

And all your moral attributes are only va-
rieties of Queensberry rules. Honor, loyalty,
purity—these are sets of regulations. The
best of you will not swerve from them: you
will die in their defense—like the gallant gentlemen you are. But you will not brook the
question whether your system of honor is
founded on right, whether loyalty has rela-

32

tion to intelligence, whether purity has relation to the state of mind. Honor means but one thing—to do the honorable thing, whether it be honor in dueling, honor among thieves, honor of women; loyalty means the quality of being loyal independent of right or wrong; purity means the chastity of the body or the denial of desire—as such; it is related to the game, not to God.

For us these distinctions do not exist, for we are serious in our intentions. We will not accept your rules because we do not understand them. Right and wrong is the only distinction we are fitted by our nature to appreciate. We are puzzled by your punctilios, your quaint distinctions, your gentleman's *comme il fauts*. We are amazed when you fight for them; we are struck dumb when you die for them—a song on your lips.

Not that *we* do not know how to die for a cause. But we must die for a serious cause, for a reason, for right, for God. Not for a slogan without meaning, for a symbol for its own sake, for a rule for its own sake. We

33

will die for the right—not for "the right
thing."

This difference in behavior and reaction
springs from something much more earnest
and significant than a difference in beliefs: it
springs from a difference in our biologic
equipment. It does not argue the inferiority
of the one or the other. It is a difference in
the taking of life which cannot be argued.
You have your way of life, we ours. In your
system of life we are essentially without
"honor." In our system of life you are essentially without morality. In your system of
life we must forever appear graceless; to us
you must forever appear Godless.

Seen from beyond both of us, there is
neither right nor wrong. There is your Western civilization. If your sense of the imper-
manence of things, the essential sportiness
of all effort, the gamesomeness and gameness
of life, has blossomed in events and laws like
these I have seen around me, it cannot, from
an external point of view (neither yours nor

The Question

ours) be classified as right or wrong. Wars for Helen and for Jenkins' ear; duels for honor and for gambling debts, death for a flag, loyalties, gallant gestures, a world that centers round sport and war, with a system of virtues related to these; art that springs not from God but from the joyousness and suffering of the free man, a world of play which takes death itself as part of the play, to be approached as carelessly and pleasantly as any other turn of chance, cities and states and mighty enterprises built up on the same rush of feeling and energy as carries a football team—and in the same ideology—this is the efflorescence of the Western world. It has a magnificent, evanescent beauty. It is a valiant defiance of the gloom of the universe, a warrior's shout into the ghastly void—a futile thing to us, beautiful and boyish. For all its inconsistencies and failures within itself, it has a charm and rhythm which are unknown to us. We could never have built a world like yours.

You Gentiles

The efflorescence of our life, given free room, is profoundly different. We have none of this joyous gamesomeness. We fight and suffer and die, even as we labor and create, not in sport and not under the rules of sport, but in the feeling and belief that we are part of an eternal process. We cannot have art such as you have, a free and careless lyrical beauty, songs and epics. Our sense of beauty springs from immersion in the universe, from a gloomy desire to see justice done in the name of God. Morality itself we take simply and seriously: we have none of your arbitrary regulations, your fine flourishes and disciplined gallantries: we only know right or wrong: all the rest seems to us childish irrelevance. When God speaks in us, when his overwhelming will drives us to utterance we are great: otherwise we are futile. With you there cannot be a question of futility. We belong to the One mastering God: you belong to the republic of playful gods.

These are two ways of life, each utterly alien to the other. Each has its place in the world—but they cannot flourish in the same soil, they cannot remain in contact without antagonism. Though to life itself each way is a perfect utterance, to each other they are enemies.

II

Sport

THE most amazing thing in your life, the most in contrast with ours, is its sport. By this I do not mean simply your fondness for physical exercise, your physical exuberance, but the psychological and social institutionalization of sport, its organization, its predominant rôle as the outlet and expression of your spiritual energies.

I will not go into the history of sports among you, contrasting it with its absence from our records and emotions. But surely there is something of extraordinary significance in the predominance of sports in your first high civilization, their religious character and their hold on the affection and attention of the masses. That the overwhelming significance of this manifestation of life has been ignored is due essentially to the pomposity of historians, who care for dignity and

Sport

"scholarship" more than for truth, and who, often lacking the shrewdness, insight, cynicism, craftiness, vulgarity, affection and livewireness, in brief, the worldliness, to understand what is going on around them in newspapers, politics and movements, think they can nevertheless understand history, which they seem to regard not as yesterday's acts of the people around them to-day, but as a detached and peculiar system, inaccessible to ordinary and uncultured intelligence. I need not go to ancient history. When I read "serious" accounts of the history of our own times, and see in what a seeming conspiracy of stupidity our historians ignore the most potent manifestation of modern life—sport, football, baseball—and concentrate almost exclusively on such trivialities as politics, which no one takes seriously, I am filled with astonishment and despair. Such men cannot write true history. But some records there are, and however small the attention which "serious" historians have given to this, we must feel that the chief free passion, that is,

the chief passion not inevitably aroused by
the struggle for existence, the chief spiritual
passion, was sport: witness the elaborate religious celebration of sporting events built
on athletic contests: witness the adulation,
the love, that was poured out to athletic
prodigies; witness the dedication of the highest, most inspired talents, to their glorification: witness the tremendous mass passions
enlisted in sporting events in Athens, in
Rome, in Byzantium and elsewhere.

But in this regard, as in most others, history is by far less important than contact with
life. I need not study history or read books
to know what sport means to you. I have
only to feel the emotions around me, read
your newspapers, watch the records of your
universities. The most certain, the most consistent, the most sustained and intense free
emotion in your life is sport. And when here
in America (as, indeed, elsewhere too) some
of your professors and educationalists deplore
and condemn the preponderating rôle of sport
in the schools, they fail to understand your

spirit. Your spirit *is* sport: particularly your young men, who are not yet absorbed in the struggle for existence, and whose emotions are therefore for the largest part free, must find in sport, in games, in contests, the most satisfactory expression of their instincts.

For the most part, of course, both professor and public, despite occasional jokes at their own expense and at the expense of the institution, sympathize with the attitude of the young and encourage it not only by their energetic interest in organized sport outside, but by the passionate attention with which they follow the sporting records of the colleges. It is a commonplace that the scholastic achievements of the universities are both unintelligible and uninteresting to the vast mass of graduates, and that academic work can in no wise compete with athletic achievement in taking the heart and interest both of these and of the general public. And even those who can understand the content of scholastic achievement are also drawn more powerfully toward sporting achievement.

41

You Gentiles

I do not agree at all with the few critics of your universities who see in this state of affairs the decline of the spirit of the country and of its educators. This state of affairs is not decadence, but the full and vigorous blossoming of your spirit. This is your way of life.

The contention of the majority of your educators, that the moral instinct is trained on the football and baseball field, in boxing, rowing, wrestling and other contests, is a true one, is truer, perhaps, than most of them realize. Your ideal morality is a sporting morality. The intense discipline of the game, the spirit of fair play, the qualities of endurance, of good humor, of conventionalized seriousness in effort, of loyalty, of struggle without malice or bitterness, of readiness to forget like a sport—all these are brought out in their sheerest and cleanest starkness in well-organized and closely regulated college sports. And on the experiences and lessons which these sports imply your entire spiritual life is inevitably founded.

Sport

It is therefore unjust to treat this aspect of your life flippantly: you yourselves often fail to recognize (except in unacknowledged instinct) how deeply it is rooted in your life. In having sundered it from the overt and organized homage which you pay to spiritual values (in the church, that is) you have split yourselves. Hence the comparative weakness of your organized churches, which are founded on a misconception. Sport *is* for you a serious spiritual matter. It is the proper symbolization, the perfect ritual, wherein your spiritual forces, finding expression, also find exercise and sustenance. They were cleaner-witted who, before the advent of Christianity, associated sport intimately with your religious life. To-day you are practising on a vast scale the troubled hypocrisy of unhappy converts who have been convinced in reason of a new religion, but whose proper and healthy instincts drive them to surreptitious homage to older gods. Were sport given its right place again in your acknowledged spiritual institution, the church, you would be happier, cleaner, stronger.

For, the premise once granted that life itself is but a joyous adventure, a combat, a passage-at-arms, you cannot do better than symbolize this premise in your athletic contests, in Olympiads, with local worship conducted on the village green and in the athletic halls and academies of the cities. The rigor of the rules (or sacred rites) which attended the open association of sport with religion testifies to the profound inner compulsion which makes the two identical. Indeed, even when religion and sport have been sundered, there is more moral odium attached to bad sportsmanship (cheating in the game, cowardice, selling out, striking foul and so on) than to the contravention of a moral injunction bearing no sporting character. You cannot, therefore, do better, from your point of view, than instil into your young a keen love and admiration of right sportsmanship, and encourage their participation in sports governed by severe regulations. Trained with sufficient consistency, they will carry into their adult life an ever-immanent sense of right and wrong according to your lights. And no better training could be devised, of course, than that which is associated with your most powerful educational institutions.

It is true that the system, even when seen from its own point of view, has its potential evils. Partisanship may become so keen that it thwarts the purpose of the sport institution. The desire to win or to be on the winning side may become so bitter as to over-rule the moral sense; and combats between champions (as once between the principals of opposing armies) may actually discourage individual participation. But every system, if it is a living thing, is subject to this danger. And even out of the evil side you may draw good. If millions watch with breathless interest the combat of champions, that combat, conducted under the truest sporting rules, becomes a great influence, and fine, gentlemanly athletes may become the teachers of the nation.

And again, seen within itself, sport-morality has as severe a discipline (if not, from our point of view, any spiritual sincerity) as a God-morality. It is as difficult and as exacting to be a gentleman as to be good. In many respects, of course, the two concepts overlap, though they are differently centered. Both call for restraint, for consideration of rules. Both are an advance on moral anarchy.

In thus characterizing your ethical concepts, I have already indicated the essential difference which separates them from ours. There is no touch of sport morality in our way of life, in our problems of human relationship. Our life morality cannot be symbolized in a miniature reproduction. We have no play-presentation of life. Our young, even like our adults, are referred at once to the first source, to the word of God, to the word of the prophet or teacher speaking in the name of God. Or, to secularize this statement, our young, like our adults, are imbued with a feeling of the absolute in their moral

46

relations. Our virtues lack the flourish and the charm of the lists: our evils are not mitigated by well-meant and delightful hypocrisies. Murder (except in self-defense) is murder, whether committed in a duel, with all its gentlemanly rules, or in unrestrained rage. When we are set face to face with an opponent, and one must kill the other, we proceed in the most effective way: we cannot understand the idea that rules of conduct govern murder. We cannot understand a man who, attacking another, insists that the other, in self-defense, shall strike only above the belt. That strange character, the gentleman thief, the gallant and appealing desperado, who recurs with such significant frequency in your fine and popular literature, perhaps points my meaning best. The idea of a "gentleman thief" is utterly impossible to the Jew: it is only you gentiles, with your idealization of the sporting qualities, who can thus unite in a universally popular hero, immorality and *Rittersittlichkeit*. It is probable, of course, that the majority of your

Robin Hoods and Claude Duvals were nothing but low ruffians, devoid even of chivalry: but their significance is not in what they were, but in what you make of them in worship. The persistence of the types is evident to-day as much as ever, when popular fancy is charmed and youth tempted into emulation by the "Raffles" and "Lupins" of the world of books. At no time have we Jews sympathized with this type. We are insensible to the appeal of "the correct" and the graceful as a substitute for our morality. Knightly or unknightly, courtly or uncourtly, sportsmanlike or the opposite in our real life mean nothing. We only ask: Is it right or is it wrong?

For the rules which you bring into life from the athletic field have no relation to the ultimate moral value of your acts and serve only to give you the moral satisfaction of having obeyed some rule or other while doing exactly what you want to do. Thus, grown and intelligent as you may be, you govern the hunting of animals with the most curious and seriously-taken regulations. You must not shoot a pigeon or a rabbit in sport unless such and such regulations are obeyed —it is "unsportsmanlike." You make a great moral to-do about these regulations. But what, in God's name, has this to do with the right or wrong of killing defenseless animals for sport?

You have attempted to infuse into business, which you have made the stark translation into modern social terms of the old kill-and-be-killed chaos, an ineffectual gallantry which will again give you the sense of "playing the game" while giving free course to your worst instincts. I mean that, apart from the necessities of the law, you attempt to bring into the field of business the curious punctilio of the fencing master—courtesies and pretenses, slogans and passwords, which mitigate only in appearance the primal savagery of the struggle. "Service," "the good of the public," "a square deal"—all the catchwords of the advertising schools which give a flavor of gamesome friendliness to a world

49

that is essentially merciless—this is not intentional lying, it is not deliberate hypocrisy. You believe that homage to these forms constitutes a morality. It does constitute a morality—of a kind. We, on our part, recognize no particular system that divides business from the rest of life. One is as honest in business as in anything else. For us business has not a specialized idealism or court etiquette, a particularized code of honor. We are honest and truthful or we are not honest and truthful: it has nothing to do with our being in "this game" or in "that game," a shopkeeper or a tailor or a banker. And because we cannot, by reason of our nature, follow you in these playful caracoles and curvetings, but drive straight to the purpose, using the plain common sense and honesty or dishonesty of the occasion, you are bound to regard us (as many of you do) as lacking in "etiquette"—that is, in your morality.

A similar division in other essential opinions illustrates the primal difference between us. Your attitude toward combat (duels, wars) and all the virtues pertaining to it, is one from which we shrink. To you courage is an end in itself, to be glorified, worshiped, as imparting morality to an act. To us, courage is merely a means to an end. Hence your courage is combative, ours passive, yours offensive, ours defensive. Heroics play a great part in your idealism—none in ours. To fight is never a glorious business to us. It is a dirty business: we perform it when we must (and I suppose there is very little to choose between you and us in the matter of courage), but we cannot pretend that the filthy necessity is a high virtue. "Dulce et decorum est pro patria mori" is not a Jewish sentiment: for it is not sweet to die for anything: but if we must die for it, we will.

Nor do we glorify the warrior as a warrior, despite occasional individual defections of ours from that view. If my brother goes mad and attacks me, and I must slay him in self-defense, how can I be happy over it? It is a cruel and miserable business, to be

finished with as soon as possible, to be for-
gotten as soon as possible. This is essentially
the Jewish attitude toward war and warriors.
I do not find in the Bible delight in war and
warriors. Our exultation in victory was not
the glorification of the warrior, but only a
fierce joy at having survived. We fought bitterly, vindictively, in order to kill: and our
God was a God of war. But however this
may be, I know with utter certainty concerning us as we are to-day that the conscious
Jew, the Jew steeped in Jewish life, despises
the fighter as such, abhors war: and though
he can die for his faith as well as any one else,
refuses to make a joyous ritual of combat.

For when you gentiles assert that you ab-
hor war, you deceive yourselves. War is the
sublimest of the sports and therefore the most
deeply worshiped. Do you mourn when you
must fight? Is a nation plunged into gloom
when a declaration of war arrives? Do you
search your hearts closely, cruelly, to discover
whether you yourselves are not to blame that
this monstrous thing has come to pass? Does

a tremor of terror go through you—"Perhaps we are guilty"? Do you clamor for the records of the long complications which have ushered in this horror? Do you go to your task of defense or offense darkly, grimly, bitterly? No, you hang out your most gorgeous banners, you play merry music, your blood runs swiftly, happily, your cheeks brighten and your eyes sparkle. A glorious accession of strength marks the throwing down or the acceptance of the gage. From end to end of the land the tidings ring out, and every man and woman of mettle—every "red-blooded" man and woman, itches for a hand in it.

Let me say clearly that I do not think all of you are fighting heroes. I have no doubt that millions of you, in every country, went to war reluctantly. But this does not contradict my contention. It only means that millions of you are not capable of living up to the ideal morality which you cherish. But even the greatest coward, even the most unwilling conscript toys, in his emotions, with

the adventures and triumphs of war. I
speak, throughout this book, of the ideals
to which you aspire and from which you
draw your moral inspiration. And it is certain that war itself, independently of all aims
and justifications, is a prime necessity to you:
and a declaration of war is the long-awaited
signal of release, greeted with extravagant
and hysterical joy. It is not love of country
which induces this flood of happiness—it is
combat, the glory of sport, the game, the
magnificence of the greatest of all contests.

Again, they were cleaner-witted, those of
you who declared openly and frankly that
war is the natural pursuit of noblemen and
of kings. The highest and most life-passion-
ate among you, the most exalted, were to be
dedicated above all others to your way of life.
Conversely, the basest among you were ac-
counted as unworthy of admittance into the
splendid company of warriors. The scullion
must not dare to aspire to combative distinction. To-day, as of old, you have nothing
but contempt (revealed in its true intensity

in time of war) for the true pacifist. Your nature is to-day what it was a thousand years ago. "In the somber obstinacy of the British worker still survives the tacit rage of the Scandinavian Berserker." And vain and futile and foolish are all these efforts to dam up and to choke the extremest and most cherished outlet of your natural instinct.

But in war, as in all other games of life, you satisfy your morality by means of amazing punctilios. To kill thus leaves you clean: to kill otherwise is ungentlemanly. In a few of these fine points in the conduct of war and of duels there may lurk some true moral significance. But it amazes us that in the exercise of this punctilio you find sufficient righteousness to ease your conscience altogether.

Were you truly concerned with right and wrong instead of with the sporting "right thing," with honor, what a flood of horror and of pity and of prostration would follow each of your wars: with what frantic haste you would fly to the consolation of each other; with what tremors of moral terror you would examine again and again the catastrophic madness from which you have just emerged. Merciful God! You have just slain ten thousand, a hundred thousand men, fathers and sons: in the red rage of combat you have disemboweled them, suffocated them, drowned them, torn them limb from limb, blinded them. A million loving parents, children, friends have wakened sweating in the night out of a terrible vision of last despairs, of contracted, screaming agonies. And now, when it is over, do you run to your churches, and with streaming eyes, fling yourselves at the foot of priest and altar, terrified lest the murder you have committed might have been avoided, lest at least some of the guilt rest upon your head? For surely if even the faintest stain of culpability, the minutest blot, a grain, an all but invisible fleck, an oversight, momentary impatience, pride, carelessness, leave you not utterly, utterly, utterly blameless, you have need of all the Divine Compassion, all the infinite forgiveness of God.

Sport

But your wars have never ended, since history records them, save with the same outbursts of pride and insolence as began them. Was there ever a Te Deum turned into a cry of Mea culpa? Was ever a war entered in a history book save as a glorious adventure, glorious in victory, glorious in disaster? And even if, after a hundred years, a historian here and there dares tarnish the stainless records of your purposes with a single plausible doubt, was there ever an awakening of guilt a thousandth part as strong as the awakening of pride and happiness which accompanies the recalling of the exploits of any war, however remote?

You have just passed through the wildest and most universal of all wars. Search your memories and your press well. Where was the hushed humility, the awe, the shuddering amazement which should have fallen on the world when the Armistice was declared? Did you not straightway send forth emissaries to bargain and barter, to accuse and to denounce? And above all to maintain your national dignity! What dignity, pray? What was left of dignity to a single one of you? What was left of decency to any who had joined in the furious and blasphemous revelries of those five years?

You hate war? Nonsense; you énjoy it. If, in the passing tiredness which follows the strenuous exertion, you pause awhile to reflect, you do not dare to think into the root-causes and evils lest indeed you make war impossible. You tinker with a few regulations, gas laws, *Flammenwerfer* rules, armed and unarmed ships and similarly futile trivialities. You call each other "bad sports"— and a day later you are prepared, if the occasion offers, to embark again on the exhilarating enterprise.

Yet, I say, for all this, you can never be guilty in your own eyes, not one of you. Denunciation can only come from one who does not share your morality. Your conscience cannot be seared, for you have done no wrong. War is the high-mark of your life, the true and triumphant expression of your instincts.

Sport

And therefore, whatever church and religion may preach in the intervals between actual fighting, you remember all your wars with wistful and longing pride as the greatest events in your existence. The splendor of war, in preparation and in action and in recollection, in the rhythm of training armies, in the frantic excitement of battle, in the glorious commemoration of monument and song and tapestry, is the flower of your civilization, material and spiritual. In nothing are you as efficient as in war; in nothing as true to yourselves. Strained to the utmost in this terrific game your splendid faculties find full and vehement exercise. And whosoever from under the shadow of God upbraids you and discourages you, is your eternal enemy.

I cannot undertake, while developing this theme, to answer all of the objections which occur even to me. In part, of course, some of these objections are unanswerable, and are, in my opinion, only overborne by counter-objections. In part they are futile objections. But in touching on some of them, I may make my viewpoint clearer. I shall be reminded that wherever war was declared we Jews have responded as readily and as eagerly as you gentiles. Statistics (which are quite reliable in such rule-of-thumb matters) bear this out. But I do not believe that we did so from motives that resembled yours. Many reasons compelled us. We are everywhere, to a large extent, aliens. A sense of inferiority in status drives us to extremes of sacrifice in justifying our claims to equality. More than that: we Jews are so frequently and so vigorously reminded, in all constitutionally governed and liberal countries, that we ought to be grateful for permission to live there, that we develop a gratitude which is not only disproportionate but occasionally grotesque. Our children, in schools and elsewhere, are taught, year in, year out, to contrast their present freedom and equality of opportunity with the oppression and bitterness which was the lot of their parents elsewhere. Frequently the contrast, as painted in their imagination, is not a duplicate of the reality. However this may be, these incessant and vehement reminders produce their effect. The child almost comes to believe that it was for the especial benefit of oppressed foreigners that America became a "free country" and, instead of accepting American forms of government level-headedly, with the proper degree of appreciation and criticism, he develops a suppressed hysteria of gratitude. This is not a healthy and natural feeling. Children should not be made to feel such things. And if it comes to the matter of contributions to liberty, we Jews have done as much for the enfranchisement of man as any other people. But the Jew, the oppressed par excellence, begins to look upon America's liberty as a personal favor. No wonder then that Jews will rush to fight for America. Yet, despite the contradiction of figures there is still a strong impression abroad that the Jews "failed in their duty," were "slackers." This feeling rises from an instinctive appreciation of that difference between us. We Jews don't like fighting. You gentiles do. Moreover, because you like fighting, you are much more skilful than we in hiding occasional reluctance to fight. Indeed, it is obvious that the more fearful you are of taking a hand in the combat, the more you will glorify and idealize it: while the Jew who is afraid adds actual and overt dislike to his cowardice.

But apart from this, we must not forget that with the schools of the Western world open to our children, *your* view of things is gradually being imposed on our alien psychology. Of the real and apparent successes of your effort I write elsewhere in this book. But here let me note that the Jewish child in your schools is made to feel that not to like fighting is a sign of complete inferiority. Determined to become your equal, he essays, often with success, to become warlike in his attitude. But it is an artificial success. He does from an imperious sense of duty what you do by instinct. He fights by forcing himself to it. He has not your natural gift and inclination for it.

62

Sport

Of course I shall be told, in establishing this distinction among others, that it is "dangerous to generalize." It is curious with what finality this commonplace is supposed to crush the generalizer. Suppose it is true that it is dangerous to generalize: are not many necessary things dangerous—like bearing children and digging coal? A truth is none the less a truth because it is a dangerous truth —i.e., open to easy abuse. Nevertheless, the most serious truths can only be stated—as generalities. And this most serious truth is among them, this contrast in attitude toward war of Jew and gentile. And as long as the contrast exists, it will be stronger than will, stronger than reason. As long as we are at opposite poles, we shall have to make continuous and strenuous efforts to get on side by side.

III

Gods

THIS is the essence of our difference: that we are serious, you are not. The French shading of the word comes nearer my meaning: *vous n'êtes pas sérieux*. Not as a matter of intent, but as a matter of constitution.

This lack of seriousness, thus uttering itself in your ethics, and governing the character of your relations to each other, must also govern your religion, your symbolized relations with the universe. And I have always felt, in contemplating your religious experiences and declarations, the same alienation from them as from your morality. Your feeling for Godhead partakes of the imaginative and lyrical playfulness which is your essential nature, and whatever may be the formal creed in which your feelings are wrapped their true nature cannot be hidden.

Gods

You gentiles are essentially polytheists and to some extent idol worshippers. We Jews are essentially monotheists. I would assert this even if it were not known that we have been singled out for centuries by our obstinate monotheism. I would assert it on the basis of my observations of the worlds I have known.

Monotheism is a desperate and overwhelming creed. It can be the expression of none but the most serious natures. It is a fundamental creed which engulfs individual and mass in an unfathomable sea of unity. In monotheism there is no room left for individual prides and distinctions, no room for joyful assertiveness. Monotheism means infinite absolutism, the crushing triumph of the One, the crushing annihilation of the ones.

To the serious nature it is inconceivable that this world should be at the changing mercy of opposing and uncontrolled forces: that gods of varying power and purpose should be making a sport of their own with us and themselves. But to the sporting na-

65

Jews are unserious on their worship of God and are actually Satanists. Number 6 is all over their symbols

6 pointed star
6 day War
& so on.

ture the ghastly unity of all life and power,
the grim and sempiternal-settled predestina-
tion of all effort is, when accessible, an intolerable thought.

We Jews are incapable of polytheism. You
gentiles are incapable of monotheism. *for Satan*

Given, in the most explicit terms, the definition of monotheism, which you have tried
as sincerely as lies in your power to accept,
you still fail to make it your own. If life here
is a sport and an heroic epic, the origins of
life must be the same. Let the exceptions
among you proclaim what they will: I know
that the creeds of your masses, as I have heard
them expounded from pulpits and in homes,
as I have read of them in books and in period-
icals, are polytheistic creeds. Of the three-
in-one, the three is stressed, the one is the reluctant concession to the dogma.

For where there is the happy and imaginative gentile spirit there cannot be the complete and unconditional prostration of the
individual. This utter breakdown of self
which is revealed in our prayers before God,

66

in our feelings towards him, is an experience which you are too proud to share. Most of our prayers are helpless repetitions of our helplessness, the stammerings of a child overwhelmed, overmastered, by contemplation of the supreme Unity. You cannot pray thus: at no time, even in the presence of the gods, do you lose your self-possession, your dignity. You too pray, but your prayers, compared with ours, are requests. Your offers of service to Christ the God are the offers of a vassal to a powerful superior. Our prayers, too, beg something, but requests of ours are folded in an abasement, a humility which would be revolting to you.

Hence it is that you have never, in these many centuries of Christianity, produced utterances like those of the prophets, of Job and of David. Your inspirations come from other sources, not from the one source. Your gods are essentially gods of the world, not of the universe. The universal aspect of divinity, its attributes of infinity and eternity, its

What universe?

67

omnipotence—these find only your formal acknowledgment: but emotionally you are unfitted to give them the true acknowledgment of complete and almost incoherent abasement. That language is alien to your spirit—the terror of the infinite cannot touch you, the eternal you know as it were by symbol and formula—but not by horrified experience. Your very professions of humility are like proud trumpet-blasts, and all your abasements of royalty, your Hapsburg burial ceremonies and anointings by priests are but artistic flourishes which bring into graceful relief the true soldierliness of your character.

I do not remember even having met the exceptions which must exist among you: I do not remember ever having heard a gentile pray with that abandonment, that abjectness, that (as it must seem to you) fulsomeness of homage which characterizes our prayer. Only they who (like us) are broken under the burden of realization of the infinite can pray thus; only they who, in dreams and in waking ecstasies and, above all, in instinct,

68

have been touched with the rage of the Undeniable Power can utter such adoration as ours.

Our very anthropomorphisms reflect the difference in our spirit. With our personified God we hold speech such as you would never hold. When we translate infinite extent into infinite individual power, we shadow forth a Being, charged with an intensity of existence, a concentration of life and force, which you are unable to apprehend, being too free in spirit to attribute to any outside force such untrammeled and unapproachable tyranny.

So your gods, too, are playthings, higher powers in the tempestuous game of life. All your mythologies were tales of adventure—for your very gods are not serious. And most fascinating are the tales of those gods which you fashioned when your first brilliant blossoming in Greece started out of your turbulent soil. Who could conceive the mythology of Greece as a product of the Jewish people? That grace, that sunny charm, that adventurousness, that quarrelsomeness—could gods

like these ever have sprung from us? The
emptiness of life and space and time brought
forth out of your free and bounding imagination a host of beings, which you imaged with
infinite loveliness in stone. One god for
heaven and one for the bowels of earth and
one for the sea, and gods for music and tragedy, gods for commerce and for voyaging—
was not this a charming game, a game of
children? Can any one say that this was a
serious and desperate attempt to become,
in concept, one with the universal spirit of
life?

Compare with this our own first gropings,
our own first clumsy expression of the universal spirit which sought utterance in us. Even
as an absolute tribal ruler our God was One,
was master, a serious God. And out of that
God-unity which we felt even in our primitive limitations, grew at last that concept
which touched with undying ecstasy the lips
of our prophets and cast over the life of the
entire people, for all time, the shadow of
omnipresence and omnipotence. Even when

Gods

our God was a jealous God, his jealousy was absolute: he would brook no homage but to him, no acknowledgment but of him. But the jealousies of your gods were only the jealousies of sport. They did not seek universal mastery and exclusiveness—only superiority. To be *primus inter pares* was the ambition of your gods, with mastery each in his own domain: but our God sought universal dominion in our hearts—such dominion as made all other homage inconceivable.

Your gods gave you loveliness and joy and battle. You liked your gods and served them with alternating loyalties: you pitted one against the other, appealed from one to the other, plotted with one against the other. Your gods were kings and princelings, mightier than you and more splendid. But no god of yours was the King of Kings in your soul. Your gods have never grown up, nor any single one among them. Nor have you grown into your god, but have always remained external, proud and warlike and free, paying homage as of old, but retaining the mastery

71

over yourselves. You do not know of a God who is *ALL*, a God in whom you are, a God who has reduced you to the dust, to the infinitesimal, in whom you are a breaking foam— a bubble on an infinite sea—it breaks: and it was born and is gone, for ever and ever.

And so, despite occasional exceptions, which I acknowledge freely, the dedication of all life, all being, to God's will and way, is alien to you. You are not naturally steeped in God. You salute him and bring him homage. Your relations with your gods are occasional, even if inevitable: but you cannot compare that with the immanence and intimacy of God-head in Jewish life. God is a common-place experience in Jewish life. He is the tacit continuous miracle of all our days and nights, thoughts and experience.

We cannot conceive of a duality—religion and life, the sacred and the secular. A Jew is a Jew in everything, not merely in prayers and in synagogue. In the eyes of a pietist, a Jew who does not follow the rules and regulations of the synagogue, who even denies all dogma is not a non-Jew: he is a bad Jew, a sinful and rebellious Jew.

In the orthodox world of Jewry, every act and incident is an acknowledged Jewish phe-nomenon: acknowledged, that is, openly, by prayer. The whole day is saturated with God, or with Jewishness. Our Jewishness is not a creed—it is ourself, our totality.

Indeed, it may be fairly said that the surest evidence of your lack of seriousness in religion is the fact that your religions are not national, that you are not compromised and dedicated, *en masse*, to the faith. For what value has God for you if you do not surrender to him, even formally, all your gifts and faculties, all your skill and emotion? This is an amazing duality of allegiance: one is an Englishman first—and then a Christian! An American first, and then a Baptist! Your most generous loyalties, your readiest sacrifices, are inspired by your nationalism. Your faculties are national: you claim, "This is typically American," "This is typically British," "This is typically French." You cut this off at once from God, and the best of yourselves you withhold from him.

But in the Jew, nation and people and faculties and culture and God are all one. We do not say: "I am a Jew," meaning, "I am a member of this nationality": the feeling in the Jew, even in the free-thinking Jew like myself, is that to be one with his people is to be thereby admitted to the power of enjoying the infinite. I might say, of ourselves: "We and God grew up together."

To have built up a great nation, millions of human beings—schools, armies, art galleries, books, legislatures, theaters, immense newspapers—is not this the all in all of national achievement, the best and strongest in you? —to have done this without your god as the central idea! Is that taking your religion seriously? No: any nation that takes its religion seriously is a nation of priests.

You will tell me that such things have been among you, that you have had national religions, national gods. I do not believe it: I have certainly seen no evidence in any record which has come to my attention. For we must distinguish between a patron or tutelary god and a national god. The first is an especially assigned power. The second is the complete reflex of the people, a god who is born with the people, who is its *raison d'être*, without whom the people would not have come into national existence. You have had patron or appropriated gods: we have a national God. In the heart of any pious Jew, God is a Jew. Is your God an Englishman or an American?

There is no real contradiction between this confessed anthropomorphism and my claim that we Jews alone understand and feel the universality of God. In anthropomorphism we merely symbolize God: we reduce the infinite, temporarily, to tangible proportions: we make it accessible to daily reference. For neither we nor you can carry on the business of ordinary living on the plane of constant abstraction. It is not because of your anthropomorphism that I accuse your religious feelings of being trivial. It is because of the manner of your anthropomorphism, it is because of what your anthropomorphism produces.

And thus, by natural reaction, we in our anthropomorphism are all the more personal because in our abstraction we are truly abstract. Because we alone are dedicated to the infinite, our God, when anthropomorphized, is our own God. I might say that there is no Jew who does not believe in God. The free-thinking Jews, the agnostic or atheistic Jew like myself, simply does not anthropomorphize him. In his religious emotions the atheist Jew is as different from the atheist gentile as the confessing Jew from the confessing gentile-Christian.

For if gods are the rationalized explanation of religious emotions they differ in acceptance and denial even as these emotions differ. And of course by "religious" emotions we only mean one aspect of all emotions. Your emotions, your life-reactions differ fundamentally from ours—why, I cannot tell. But as in morality you are freer, sporting and

76

variegated, so your gods are many, varied and manly. And our gloomy and merciless monotheism, intolerant in abstraction and in personification, is the eternal enemy of your gods.

IV

Utopia

THE dreams of men concerning the latter
days are a common index to their ideals of
life, for no one will think of the future except
as his own. These dreams, like their close
kin, the night dream, are extraordinarily difficult of interpretation—much more difficult
than the psychoanalyst would have us believe. But on occasions they are presented
with unmistakable clarity and directness—by
the prophets.

The functions of the prophet as a seer and
a foreseer have been confounded for this reason. The true prophet sees into the ultimate
longings of his group—longings which may
even run counter to the day's desires. These
ultimate longings are shifted into the far future—beyond the reach of temporal complications and compromises: and he that unveils

78

Utopia

a man's inmost longings wins credence as having foreseen the true finality of life.

I have chosen Plato's Republic and our own Hebrew prophets as the basis of contrast between your dreams of the latter days and ours, between your longings for perfection and ours. I have chosen Plato because of all the seers who have sprung up in your midst he is the most universally accepted, and of all Utopias your thinkers refer to his most frequently: that is to say, he comes nearest to your desires. Hence in discussing him, I am discussing you.

I have used the phrase "of all the seers who have sprung up in your midst" because it is true that you still mention the Hebrew prophets more frequently than Plato. But it is of singular and final significance that as soon as you develop free intelligence and desire expression for it, you turn from our prophets to your own. The overwhelming bulk of your intelligent discussion of life and the end of life centers round the free philosophers or seers—and among these you have made Plato preëminent. Plato's analysis of the ideal life still approaches your dreams most intimately.

Investigating the true nature of morality, Plato bodies forth his ideal of a perfect state, and, with the license of a dream giving free reign to his imagination, unfolds step by step his famous Republic. No considerations of practicality or of feasibility were there to check the career of his fantasy. The Republic is to him life as it should be and as he would like to see it: the apotheosis of human aspiration.

Contrast this with the visions of his almost contemporaries, the Jewish prophets, and in this contrast you will find again the key to our essential difference.

The Republic of Plato is an institution, organized with infinite ingenuity and dedicated to the delights of the body and the mind. It draws its inspiration from the pure *joi de vivre* of the ideal man of perfect physical and psychic health. You would seek in vain that extraneous compulsion of a God which the Hebrews called inspiration. There is no somber passion driving to creation, no intolerant demands impossible of fulfilment. It is not God creating man in his mold: it is man creating God, or the gods, in *his* mold: gods that are companionable and comprehensible.

He sets before you a pretty, intriguing little model ("a city not too big to lose the characteristics of a city") which, sundered from universal humanity, untouched by the universal hunger, restricts Supreme Good to the possession of a comfortably secluded group. It is a city for the prosecution of the happy and artistic life; the harmonies and symmetries shall be carefully guarded, the satisfaction of body and of mind wisely and cleverly pursued. Nay, in that supreme human product there shall even be—astounding triviality—a censor!

There is a wealth of ingenuity devoted to these questions: How shall children be initiated into the art of war? How shall cowards and heroes be treated? What about

81

the plundering of the slain, and the perpetuation of deeds of battle in monuments? "Now, is it not of the greatest moment that the work of war shall be well done? Or is it so easy that any one can succeed in it and be at the same time a husbandman or a shoemaker or a laborer or any other trade whatever, although there is no one in the world who could become a good draught player or dice player by merely taking up the game at unoccupied moments, instead of pursuing it as his special study from childhood? And will it be enough for a man merely to handle a shield or any other of the arms and implements of war, to be straightway competent to play his part well that very day in an engagement of heavy troops or in any other military service? . . ."

"Is it not of the greatest moment that the work of war should be well done? . . ." This in a vision of human perfection—for it never occurs to Plato that perfection in humanity precludes the possibility of war.

And treating of God, he says: "Surely God is *good* in reality, and is to be so represented," but what can we make of his ultimate good? Is not his good merely "a good thing"—as right is for you "the right thing"? And what can we make of his God when, after talking of the goodness and dignity of God, he goes on to talk of the gods, and of how the poets are to be arraigned for not treating them respectfully in that they make them laugh or portray them in undignified occupations and postures!

Well does he say: "The inquiry we are undertaking is no trivial one, but demands a keen sight." He does not say that it demands the aid of God, or a loving heart, or hunger after righteousness. But the very question of God is a trivial one, for, as one says in this book: "It is urged neither evasion nor violence can succeed with the gods. Well, but if they either do not exist, or do not concern themselves with the affairs of men, why need *we* concern ourselves to evade their observation?"

This graceful skepticism, which strikes the opening note of the book, sets the tone for the entire theme. "What is justice?" What indeed? Does any man that loves true justice (not the game) ever ask this question? Can any one truly believe that the subtlest and skilfulest analysis of justice will help one jot in creating love of justice, desire for justice?

A vision of the perfection of mankind and children being trained for war! Contrast it with this: "In that day there shall be a highway out of Egypt to Assyria, and the Assyrian shall come into Egypt, and the Egyptian into Assyria, and the Egyptians shall serve with the Assyrians. In that day shall Israel be the third with Egypt and with Assyria, even a blessing in the midst of the land. Whom the Lord of hosts shall bless, saying: Blessed be Egypt my people and Assyria the work of my hands and Israel mine inheritance." Or with the better known passage: "And it shall come to pass in the last days that the mountain of the Lord's house shall be established on the top of the mountains, and shall be exalted above the hills, and all

nations shall flow into it. And many peoples
shall come and say: Come, let us go up to
the mountains of the Lord, to the house of the
God of Jacob, and he will teach us of his
ways and we will walk in his paths. . . . And
he shall judge the nations and shall rebuke
many peoples, and they shall beat their
swords into ploughshares, and their spears into
pruning hooks: nation shall not lift up sword
against nation, neither shall they learn any
more war."

A vision of the perfection of mankind, with
censors and with carefully groomed gods!—
the limit of his imagination. But this!—
"And the earth shall be filled with the knowledge of God as the waters cover the sea."
And this!—"And it shall come to pass after-
ward that I will pour out my spirit upon all
flesh, and your sons and your daughters shall
prophesy: your old men shall dream dreams.
Your young men shall see visions. And also
upon the servants and upon the handmaids
in those days will I pour out my spirit."

You Gentiles

And because his world is not God's world, but the world of his self-created gods, he must sit down and argue anxiously, "What is justice?" But he that really loves justice asks no questions: he cries instead: "Seek good and not evil, that ye may live: and so the Lord, the God of Hosts, shall be with you, as ye have spoken. Hate evil and love the good, and establish judgment in the gate." And: "Let judgment run down as waters and righteousness as a mighty stream."

And when, baffled by the inadequacy of his human standards, your philosopher refers justice to the "categoric imperative," he betrays the triviality of your world. What is that "categoric imperative," that helpless compromise and confession? What man recognizes it, will bow to it? That phrase itself is its own denial, for he that refers mankind to a "categoric imperative" is himself neither categoric nor imperative. But even the deaf will hear and tremble when the Prophet thunders: "Thus saith the Lord." *There* is the categoric imperative!

Utopia

For me, conscious of being Jewish and of the meaning of being Jewish, it is impossible to write of this contrast without bias, as if this book were merely an intellectual exercise. Because I am Jewish I look with ultimate aversion on the world which finds supreme and ideal expression in Plato's Republic. And though I may repeat that this is no question of right and wrong in these two worlds, yours and ours, I cannot but feel profoundly and vehemently that ours is the way and the life.

Yet I would pay what tribute I can to the dreams of one like Plato. I have at least touched your world closely enough to have caught some of the beauty of its freedom.

There is a Jewish legend which tells that when God brought the Law, his Law, to the children of Israel assembled at the foot of Sinai, after he had offered it to all the other peoples, only to have it rejected, he left them no choice, but said: Either you take my Law or I will lift up this mountain and crush you beneath it. I attach no psychological significance to the fable (the practice of interpreting fables psychologically is, as a rule, a dishonest one), but quote it as a handy illustration. We are not free to choose and to reject, to play, to construct, to refine. We are a dedicated and enslaved people, predestined to an unchangeable relationship. Freedom at large was not and is not a Jewish ideal. Service, love, consecration, these are ideals with us. Freedom means nothing to us: freedom to do what?

Yet in glimpses I understand the charm of your life and sometimes lose myself in the fascination of your Plato's dream. Such a world as he foreshadows, a world of sunlight, exercise, singing, fantasy: a world of graceful and elastic bodies, of keen, flashing minds, of clash and effort, wars and heroes and monuments, a life wheeling and dashing in splendid formations, rejoicing under free and lovely skies: a life without brooding and gloom, without the intolerable burden of this unrelaxing immanence. Man and man's effort, man's love and agonies are ends in themselves, to be exploited for themselves: the coming and going of men and nations and gods are without ultimate significance, a dance of atoms, a passing ecstasy without thought of the sinister beyond. Beautiful—but not for us! While this dance goes on, while nations and gods enter the game and leave it, we continue through all time, an apparition almost, a dread reminder of infinity.

Your dreams of perfection are only of a piece with your present life—the transient become permanent: the skies will be blue forever, your dance will never end. Your bodies will always be strong, your wits keen, your battles glorious: the game will reach its limit of enjoyment!

But for us this is not an apotheosis: this is not a vision. For us the end is ecstatic unity, the identification of man with God. Your ideal is eternal youth, ours lifts toward an unchanging climax of adult perfection. You would like to play with your gods forever: we will return to God, to the universe. Yours is a sunlit afternoon, with the combatants swaying forever in a joyous struggle. Ours is a whole world, with the spirit of God poured through all things.

Your ideal is Plato's Republic: ours is God's kingdom.

V

Loyalty

WHENEVER friendly tribute has been paid to the higher ethical nature of the Jew, it has always been made to appear that the Jew obeys the laws of a common morality more strictly than does the gentile. Jews and friends of Jews have wanted to make it appear that, if we differ from you ethically, it is in that we are more self-sacrificing, more generous, more loyal, more honest, etc. I do not desire to make it appear so, and in the foregoing pages I have tried to avoid any such implication. Within our system we need be neither better nor worse behaved than you within yours. We may transgress as frequently as you, perhaps more frequently—I cannot tell: it is on the nature of the systems that I base the distinction. We deny your very system, you ours.

You Gentiles

So that, casually, we must seem immoral to you, you to us. That is why even the lowest type of gentile despises the Jew; the lowest type of Jew, the gentile. For it is well to remember that criminals do not deny a system of ethics: they only transgress it. To the criminal the subverter of a system of morality is a horrible creature, as (which I have already intimated) to the coward the pacifist is particularly abhorrent. This must spring from the fact that for the professional criminal it is essential that humanity should be moral: his very existence as a criminal would otherwise be impossible. Indeed, he has more reason than any one else to foster a sense of morality in mankind, for the more exceptional he is, the better for his trade. Hence his greatest enemy is not the policeman (for the policeman maintains the social order which is his prey), but the moral anarchist. And since the Jew is to the gentile order of conduct a moral anarchist, the gentile criminal who has come into contact with Jews will be the aptest to hate Jews. It is for this reason, I think, that criminality is so closely allied to anti-Semitism.

In the attitude of the public toward literary and stage censorship I find the clearest illustration of this distinction between the breaking of law and the denial of law. A play which is "indecent" may be so for one of two reasons. Either it deals with sex within the frame of morality or it denies the validity of this morality. In the first case (which covers most successful plays) we have no attack on current notions of what is right and wrong in the sexual relationship. We have, indeed, complete acceptances of the current principles of sex morality. But with this acceptance *en principe* goes a generous denial in practice; plays of this kind cover countless breaches of morality with a knowing wink, a tolerant appeal to human weakness. It is ludicrous to deny that the desire to tickle and provoke the sexual appetite, and covertly to encourage its promiscuous satisfaction, governs these plays; but it is not made a principle at all. It is the breaking of the law, not the denial of it. Hence such plays (except when they become too obvious in their purpose and thus become an overt attack *en masse*) are tolerated by the censorship and encouraged by the public.

But the play which has little sex appeal yet seriously denies the validity of accepted sex morality is dealt with promptly and severely, and among those who condemn it most vigorously will be found those who frequent assiduously the first type of play. I see nothing incongruous in this—nothing illogical even. For the first type of play is perhaps the safety valve to human nature: it remits us our unavoidable allowance of licence, without which morality would become an insufferable imposition. But the second type of play breaks up morality completely. To the system of law the amoralist is more dangerous than the criminal. The naked chorus-girl is less dangerous than the naked truth. Such a danger—a danger not merely of malpractice, but of essential denial —is the Jew in your morality. And against

the Jew there is a *Union Sacrée* of all classes
and conditions of men, the prince, the laborer, the professor, the saint, the thief, the
prostitute, the soldier, the merchant. There
does not seem to be a single country with a
history which has not been anti-Semitic at
one time or another. There is no country to-
day of which the Jew can say, "In this country anti-Semitism will never become triumphant." Your dislike of us finds uneven and
unequal expression, is lulled into rest for a
time, at times is overborne by generous impulses, but it is a quality inherent in the nature of things, nor is it conceivable to me
that, as long as there are Jews and gentiles, it
should ever disappear.

For your system of morality is no less a
need to you than ours to us. And the incom-
patibility of the two systems is not passive.
You might say: "Well, let us exist side by
side and tolerate each other. We will not attack your morality, nor you ours." But the
misfortune is that the two are not merely
different. They are opposed in mortal,

though tacit, enmity. No man can accept both, or, accepting either, do otherwise than despise the other.

No single attribute or virtue shows our mutual enmity more clearly than that of loyalty, which, among all the attributes contributing to your morality, is perhaps the most dearly cherished, the most vehemently advocated. It is impossible for me, in writing of it, to take up a purely analytic attitude; but I believe that the preferences and aversions which I here express will at least serve to make clear the irreconcilable difference between Jewish and gentile morality.

The abstraction, loyalty, is not related to good and bad. Loyalty is preached naked, as a virtue for itself. It is proper and right to be loyal. To do a thing out of loyalty— loyalty to a man, to a group, to an idea—is in itself a sort of justification. To develop a loyalty is in itself commendable.

To the Jew, naked loyalty is an incomprehensible, a bewildering thing. That men should be called upon to keep a quantity of this virtue on constant tap, to be applied on instruction to this or that relationship, is not merely irrational to us: it is beyond the apprehension of our intelligence.

We can understand love born of a natural relationship. But the quality of love differs essentially from the quality of loyalty. Loyalty is demanded as an independent quality, as a thing in itself; it is cultivated (love cannot be "cultivated"); it is stimulated and forced. It is not demanded, essentially, that you love: it is demanded that you be loyal.

Very often, indeed, loyalty is demanded where a demand for love would be too obviously ludicrous. For the application of loyalty is to you as seemly in the case of an association of shoe salesmen as in the case of country itself.

It is expected, in your world, that a man should be loyal to his country, to his province, to his city, to his section of the city, to his college, to his club, to his business associations, to his fraternity, to every chance group into which events may bring him. In the first

97

instance, country, the distinction between love and loyalty is startlingly clear. Love of country is a profound spiritual quality: it may go hand in hand with a dangerous and exalted morality. But loyalty merely says: "My country must triumph in all her undertakings, whether they be right or wrong"—or, rather, "There is no such thing as 'my country wrong.'" And in loyalty to king, class, or church, the same distinction or substitution is observed. Loyalty is a rigid code of behavior—not an emotion.

But the real nature of loyalty is only seen in its application to those relationships which are much more fortuitous than those of country, church, class. In these loyalty is clearly revealed as a fictitious and artificial regulation, with no roots in moral conviction. Let us take the case of a young man who is faced with a choice of college. He may have preferences, but there is no compelling association which identifies him with any one institution. The choice is decided finally by some quite irrelevant influence: he goes to any one college as he might have gone to any other. But once he is there loyalty demands that he regard this college as the best in the country —perhaps in no particular, for particulars are occasionally too tangible—but at large; the best, the finest, the noblest. Of this college he must think, and above all speak, with enthusiasm, passion and devotion; he must defend its name against all aspersions, without investigating their foundations: if he even stops to consider the plausibility of these aspersions before denouncing them, the quality of his loyalty is already second-rate. The scholastic reputation of his college may be less than mediocre; its staff may not number a single scholar of note; its alumni may be an indistinguishable mob of obscure failures: worst of all, its football and baseball teams may be the laughing-stock of the locality. But his college is the best and noblest in the country and the world: the astonishing feature of all this being that not only his schoolmates expect him to say and seem to believe so, but that everybody outside the college, convinced of its worthlessness, also expects this of him and considers him rather a cad if he acquiesces in what to them may be obviously true.

This obligation of loyalty must pursue the man to the end of his life. Forty years after he has left his college he will be regarded with suspicion as something less than a gentleman if he should have discovered that his Alma Mater was and is an extremely inferior and uninteresting institution: "It may be all that, you know, but a man's got to be loyal to his college."

What is true of college loyalty is true of other loyalties. A man who joins the army and is assigned to any regiment must have loyalty for his regiment—which means that he must seem to lose the faculty of discrimination and criticism as soon as the regiment he was accidentally assigned to is under consideration. Should he in later life become a member of a fraternity, of a business association, of a poker-club, he must be loyal. He must be loyal even at large, without an organ-

Loyalty

ization to be loyal to. He must be loyal to the paper-manufacturing trade, to the cleaners and dyers, to the transport business. And if he goes down into a factory to earn, by the sweat of his brow and under bitter duress, a bare livelihood, he must at once be loyal to his employers.

But the application of loyalty is sometimes pushed to extremes which are nothing short of grotesque. One finds in surface cars notices like these: "Be loyal to the Bronx, to Bensonhurst, to Wapping, to Pendleton, to Charlottenburg, to the Ring, to the Marshalkowska, to Montmartre. . . ." Sometimes I have wondered: "If you live in the Bronx and are loyal to your neighborhood grocer, how long are you supposed to yearn for him after you have moved to Brooklyn: and how soon may you with seemliness develop a loyalty for your neighborhood grocer in Brooklyn? Or are you supposed to leap into your loyalties at once as into a bath-tub and be immersed in them without a moment's loss? And similarly, how if you attend two or three colleges in succession, or are attached to a number of regiments in succession? Or change your business, or your fraternity or your poker-club?"

It is clear to me that the very quality of loyalty and its place in your life again bespeaks the sport origin of your morality. The success of a football team depends not only on the physical aptitude and fitness of its members, but also on their spirit, their *esprit de corps*. There must be atmosphere for sporting effect: it is as important as physique and must be cultivated as assiduously, as carefully, as skilfully, as artificially. Whichever team you join, your loyalty is essential to its success and your loyalty must be instantaneous and unconditional, neither curtailed by delay nor mitigated by reflection. Your loyalty has nothing to do with ultimate moral values. It is part of the game—and life is to you a game, on the football field, in the college, in the factory, on the battlefield. "The Game" alone can make loyalty a transportable quality of this kind. "The Game"

102

alone can give birth to the concept of loyalty.

In our life, the Jewish life, loyalty is unknown. There is no equivalent for it among our attributes. We understand love, which is serious, profound: which must be treated, therefore, with due dignity. But we do not understand loyalty, which is trivial, gallant, gamesome, conventionalized.

As students, we Jews are accused of lacking the right attitude toward the college. It is perfectly true that we have not the "loyal" attitude—as you have it, or, despite occasional efforts, to the degree in which you have it. We are apt to see the college as an institute of learning: we go there to study under competent teachers. What has loyalty to do with this organization? We may develop love for the place: it may, in later years, become a beloved memory, or it may not. But we cannot attach an immediate combative value to our connection with the college—an instantaneous regimental pride: we cannot attach a moral value to the prescribed set of sporting emotions and thrills

which are supposed to be a proper part of
college life. We are unquestionably an alien
spirit in your colleges. For your colleges are
the most coherent mouthpieces of your morality: and that morality is not ours. Your college is a miniature world in which you first
develop the sporting instincts which must ac-
company you through the real world. We
(with our proper exceptions) see the college
only as a center of study, and, incidentally,
occasionally of valued friendships. The idea
of a rivalry with other colleges, in which each
student must defend his own college, seems
to us childlike. It is not to the purpose at
all. It is not serious.

But I have touched on the college only as
a single illustration of the predominance of
the virtue of loyalty in your concept of the
proper human relationship. All your society
is divided into "teams"—with a fictitious
morality to correspond. It has little to do
with direct utilitarianism. One might object,
saying: "This morality, like any other, is
merely the adjunct of the economic or biologic

struggle. What we call 'morality' is merely the assistant illusion in the struggle for existence. And in this regard gentile and Jew are alike." But this is an irrelevant truth. There was a time when, among you gentiles, one man would courteously challenge another to mortal combat: without real motive, without enmity, without passion. So it was: when no excuse for combat was available you dropped even the pretense of an excuse. Do not answer that this was a passing phase: for I say that when men actually kill each other for mere sport it betokens a profound, an almost eternal instinct. That instinct to-day finds expression in equally moralless relations, equally passionless associations and enmities. You arrange your life in such wise as to get the maximum of sport out of it. And, for the purpose of sport, it does not matter to which team you belong: England or America, Harvard or Yale, the Black Watch or the Old Guard, the Neighborhood Association of Wigan or the Rotarians of Los Angeles, the Goodrich Rubber Factory or the Sunlight

You Gentiles

Soap Garden City, the Alpha Sigma Mu or the '95 Club, the Progressive Republicans or the Decorators' Association, the United Cigar-makers or the Fascisti. There's good fun in all this; it is exciting, jolly, sporty. It puts rush and gaiety into life. But we Jews are no good at it. Just as we are inaccessible to the meaningless exhilaration of college loyalty, so we are bewildered by the fast and furious games of your general life. We Jews cannot play the game.

Perhaps you will answer that it is you who, taking the chance relationships of life as the all-in-all of existence, are really serious: that it argues seriousness in a man if he gives to every passing association all faculties, all his emotion. Such an argument would be a quibble. A woman may take an absorbing interest in dress—to the exclusion of everything else: one could hardly call her serious. Serious absorption in trivialties is not seriousness. Then you may answer me: "But all life is a triviality"—which would reveal clearly the difference between your outlook and ours.

VI

Discipline

ONE of the best illustrations wherewith to contrast your adaptability to discipline and our lack of it is to be found in the difference between your behavior in church and our behavior in our own unmodernized synagogue— the orthodox synagogue.

In church all is order and decorum, rhythm and régime. In the synagogue all is chaos. In the church leaders and responses are carefully prepared, carefully followed and observed. It is clean and neat, charming and exact. You behave well. You do as you are told—in mass. You create *esprit de corps* in the church: there is a suggestive, hypnotizing decency in the trained correctness of your service. In the synagogue all is disorder; we talk during service; we answer out of turn; and when we answer in mass one begins earlier, another ends later;

it is Babel itself; people walk in and out; some take longer than others to get through a certain prayer—and the ones who read more rapidly chat in the interval; part of the congregation is standing, part sitting; some wear prayer shawls, others do not: and the prayer shawls are not all alike; sometimes there is so much babbling that the voice of the cantor or leader cannot be heard. One of you at our services would be amazed: our own young generation, which has picked up your ways, is disgusted: and the last couple of generations has seen Reform synagogues conducted on your models.

Taking this illustration (as one fairly may) of model discipline and lack of it, we may say, as is often said: "You gentiles are disciplined; we Jews are not." And it is not in church and synagogue alone that we find this contrast. It persists, equally clear cut, in all branches of organized life. Compare any gentile institution with an uncorrupted corresponding institution in Jewish life and you will observe it. At your secular public as-

Discipline

semblies the same decency and unified restraint; at ours, the same scrambling irregularity. Jewish meetings never begin on time, never end on time. In your clubs and societies—order and harmony; in ours, noise, disorder and wastage. Your programs are observed with fair strictness; our programs are merely *points de départ*. In your homes calm and even systematization; in ours boisterous affections, formlessness.

And despite much effort we cannot introduce your rhythmic exercise of discipline into our life—and retain our individuality. We can imitate you—excellently: produce a substitute as good as the original. But the institution then no longer has Jewish spirit: it is a gentile institution artificially maintained by Jews—like our Reform Temples—and in these the Jew gradually learns to present a gentile exterior. But wherever we are unrestrainedly Jewish we shock you by our uncouthness. We lack social grace—the disciplined and distinguished social grace of high society, as well as the mean and spiritless punctiliousness of your middle classes. In the colleges, in the street, in the surface cars, in the clubs, in the army, we betray ourselves. Indeed, your very breaches of discipline differ from ours by a certain conscious rebelliousness which is partly homage: our breaches of discipline are off-hand, unconscious, insolent.

And carrying this still further, we Jews, the most clannish of peoples, are helplessly disorganized—we have never achieved comparative unity, not even in a single territory— much less throughout the world. All our organizations are small, but never too small to be unwieldy because of dissension and, worse than dissension, because of unamenability to regular discipline. To those who have known the comparative evenness of your organizations, political, religious, social, commercial, we are an unsightly people: and every effort to impose this sense of form on us only accentuates our formlessness.

This distinction between us again points to the root difference between us—your triviality and our seriousness. The fact is, of course, that in true discipline, in effectiveness, we are by no means your inferiors. No one would dream of asserting that our religion is not more effective than yours in compelling obedience, or in perpetuating itself. The mere fact that we have persisted for eighty generations in maintaining a racial and spiritual identity in the face of so much persecution (and, more significant, of so much infiltration of blood) bespeaks essential discipline of amazing rigor and power. Disorganized as we are, we have outlived the most ably organized nations. We have failed to imitate the Roman legion or the Order of Jesus: we have survived the first and shall no doubt outlive the second. We have not your skill, your German, or English, or American skill in wheeling perfectly vast masses of perfectly subordinated men. Yet I have no doubt that when Germany and England and America will long have lost their present identity or name or purpose, we shall still be strong in ours.

111

You Gentiles

For true discipline should always be seen in relation to a purpose. Your discipline is goose-step discipline: it is the hypnotic discipline of imposing rhythms, possible only in the absence of the individual discipline. There is hypnotic charm in your discipline—but it is not effective; as soon as the organization crumbles, the individuals are lost. We have never been the victims of organization.

Your organization-discipline, moreover, is a necessary part of your sport life. Games cannot be conducted without discipline: discipline is the essence of a game: when two perfectly disciplined beings are opposed, the game is at its best. And the same feeling runs through all your manifestations of life: the game of nationalisms, the game of society, the game of commercial success.

The most startling and compelling monuments of your gentile genius are not individual productions—but the productions of mass. Most of the wonders of the ancient world were wonders springing out of great organ-

Discipline

ized rhythmic effort and your chief wonders to-day, those which dominate your general life, are like these. Great buildings; great countries; great ships; great wars; the pyramids, the Olympic, the Colossus of Rhodes, the Hanging Gardens, the Eiffel Tower and the Woolworth building, the Red Cross, the Catholic church, Babylon, New York, the Daily Mail—these are the distinctive triumphs of your civilizations, the final appeal. And individual ingenuity is subordinated to the production of your mass effects, your discipline-monsters. What single individuals can alone effect plays a very minor rôle in your way of life. Mass and rhythm and team work—the game: this is your ideal.

It is not ours: and we are impressed only superficially and transiently by these productions. The individual is our climax, as the mass is yours. A hundred thousand men labored for twenty years to build the great pyramid: one man wrote the book of Isaiah. You will answer: "One man also wrote 'Hamlet' and the 'Critique of Pure Reason' and the

113

You Gentiles

'Republic.' " But I ask: Are Plato and Shakespeare and Kant in your life what the Bible, the Talmud, the rabbis are in ours? To our very masses, the Jewish masses, the wonders of the world are Moses, Elijah, the Rambam, the Vilna Gaon, the Dubna Maggid, the chassid in the neighboring village. These actually dominate our life, as governments, mass radio exploits, armies and Woolworths dominate yours. We are the people of the Book. But we were the people of the Book before a million copies could be printed in a single day.

This intractability of ours to your disciplines is one of our chief and (to you) most unpleasant characteristics. It is best noticeable in our new arrivals in Western countries, those who, in Eastern ghettos, have lived a more nearly Jewish life: it is much less noticeable in our modernized types—though here still noticeable; for, despite our clever imitativeness, we do retain our natural character and cannot hide it consistently, but betray ourselves at intervals. In the colleges, in the army (least here, except during the great war,

Discipline

for in peace-time only the Westernized Jews join the army), in business associations, we irritate and disgust you by our obdurate seeming singularity. We don't fit in properly. We don't keep a straight line on the social or public parade; we don't cheer in unison; we don't bow with the waving of the wand. We don't play the game.

This is comprehensibly irritating in the highest degree, and in your irritation you have ascribed these infractions to our savagery. You have said we are not fit for civilization. We have not the ability to subordinate the individual to the community: or, if we have the ability, we have not the desire, not having the ethical impulse. With us, you have said, it is every man for himself. We are too impudent, individually; we cannot behave as gentlemen should—unobtrusively, submissive to the code, tacit, unassertive, regular.

This is what you mean, saying we are undisciplined.

But the fact is that we consciously despise

the code itself. It is not that we recognize its validity and refuse to submit to it out of individual and selfish reasons: it is rather that the whole game disgusts us—and your seriousness in it, most of all. It is to us a ludicrous, and not an impressive thing, to see ten thousand grown-up men, a large proportion of them actually fathers, marching in step up and down a street or across a field. This blaring of the trumpets, this beating of the drums, this Left-Right-Left-Right, this rhythmic, snappy form-fours, this intoxication of united mass movement, which sends you gentiles frantic with excitement is a laughable exhibition to us. "Foolish gentiles!" we say contemptuously. To us ten thousand fools are not more impressive than a single fool. Where you see the flash of swinging ranks, a mighty lifting and falling, power, magnificence, we see only ten thousand serious-faced men engaged in astonishing antics, with astonishing skill.

The drill of your regiments, the drill of your colleges, of your social usages, your clubs, all impress us alike with their triviality. We do not understand it.

Perhaps you will reply that this contempt is merely rationalization. We despise discipline because we lack it and secretly we aspire to acquire it. But in fact it is the most severely disciplined Jew who most heartily despises your disciplines. It is the modernized Jew, who has thrown off the discipline of orthodox Judaism, who comes nearest your spirit. It is the orthodox Jew, the most Jewish Jew, who least understands you.

And it is this orthodox Jew, this ghetto Jew, whose apparent individualism deprives his mass life of all form and discipline, it is this orthodox Jew who seems, of all Jews, to be least accessible to your orderliness, it is this orthodox Jew who nevertheless submits to an amazing discipline unknown to most of you. I have said that the obstinate maintenance of our identity and our religion through eighty generations of oppression bespeaks a rigorous and effective discipline. But what that discipline is in practice you do not real-

ize. The orthodox Jew submits to an unrelaxing régime which you gentiles would find
intolerable. It governs him in all his actions,
from birth to death; it controls and directs,
with an iron hand, his daily occupations: it
pervades, with obsessive immanence, every
moment of his time, every movement, every
function. The orthodox Jew begins the day
with long prayer, closes it with long prayer:
he cannot take a glass of water without a
prayer, he cannot satisfy his physical needs
without a prayer. He stops for long intervals, afternoon and evening, to pray. The
discipline extends to his relations with his
wife; it imposes on him the obligation of
study; it binds him to daily and hourly use
of a language—Hebrew—artificially maintained; it intersperses his years with numer-
ous fasts and feasts, each with its enormous
burden of ritual and tradition. All this over
and above the fierce discipline of the world's
enmity and contempt, the discipline of mere
existence in an alien and unfriendly atmosphere.

Discipline

Much of this religious ritual covers eventualities which you would regard as secular; dietetic laws, sanitary laws, sex laws, social laws: for *all* life is religion to the Jew, and *all* life, proceeding from God, must be governed by him. But when the ritual is reduced to what even you would call the religious, it still presents a bulk of tyranny to which you would never submit, a discipline which you are incapable of suffering: a discipline which demands incessant vigilance, lest a prayer be omitted, a discipline the details of which it takes years to acquire and into which one must be trained from childhood.

And what is most relevant in this connection is that this discipline is a corporate discipline—it is directed to a common purpose outside of the individual, to the perpetuation of a people through its religion. In our religious ideology the selfish salvation of the individual soul is a very minor theme. It is, I believe, an acquired dogma, and its irrelevance is proved by its unimportance. Our

119

prayers are largely common prayers; we pay little attention to the after life—and even our dreams of an after-life are associated with the Jewish people as a whole. As individuals we sometimes pray for personal benefits—but so infrequently that we could omit these prayers without changing the bulk of our ritual; most of our prayers are prayers of glorification: they link the people as a whole to God. They re-dedicate the people as a whole to God's service; they praise God for the burdens he has placed upon us—and, with passionate iteration, they thank him for having made us different from you.

It does not need a Jewish scholar—it needs only an intelligent Jew who has lived in an orthodox or semi-orthodox environment—to appreciate that all this tyranny of discipline was bent to one end—to our preservation as a distinct and separate people. We feel that we are not merely different from you at points: it is a totality of difference and of separation. We have carried out with us into

120

Discipline

exile the complete atmosphere of our national
life: our holy festivals are largely national,
and even in those which are predominantly
religious there is the continuous, minor theme
of our separate nationalism. One holiday
celebrates the liberation of the Jewish people
from Egypt, another the deliverance of the
people from the Asiatic-Greek oppressor, another the confusion of a national enemy, still
others celebrate the time of the Palestinian
harvest (the irony and tragedy of it!) with
appropriate prayers and ceremonies: and even
in our "pure" religious festivals the memory
of our national institutions, our Temple, our
hereditary priesthood, maintains an unbroken
background of suggestion.

And with these recurrent climaxes in our
religious life dominated by the national consciousness, the general tenor of all our religion repeats this theme from day to day.
The discipline of our religion, of our Jewishness, is a corporate discipline, the subjection
of the individual to the mass. I repeat this

to remind you that, contrary to your accusation, the intractability of the Jew to your forms of discipline does not spring from individualism or from lack of a social con-science. We are disciplined more bitterly than you, and we bear the discipline without the assistance of narcotic rhythms: we bear our burden like civilized adults.

Nor do I see any contradiction between this fierce insistence on separate national exist-ence and our dedication to a universal ideal. We believe and feel that for such an ideal we alone, as a people, possess the especial apti-tude. The orthodox Jew bases it on divine will and choice: others, like myself, know not on what to base it (a special racial psychol-ogy, the result of inbreeding, the result of accident)—but believe it none the less. We shall not further that ideal by losing our iden-tity; to mingle with you and be lost in you would mean to destroy the aptitude, for ever. Thus universal ideal and national identity are inextricably bound up. To the maintenance of this high union we have given, consciously,

Discipline

seriously, without kings and courts, without medals and reviews and Orders, without cheering and without drills, a bitter and obstinate devotion more exacting than anything you have known and, in its deliberate effects, more successful.

VII

The Reckoning

I HAVE spoken of Jews and gentiles—in mass. Certain of you will assuredly object: "You cannot deal with masses as with men. 'You cannot indict a nation.'"

The objection is futile—not only has it been the universal practice to indict and to punish masses as if they had personality and to treat nations as such: but you are doing it to-day, everywhere. And I believe that fundamentally, the practice is just, despite the objections of the few whom I shall answer here. Particularly consonant is the practice with your gentile philosophy. Here is your nation: X. It is composed of militarists and pacifists and mobs. The government is militaristic—whether it represent a minority or a majority. And the militaristic government engages the whole country in its acts: is responsible for a war, for oppression. How shall we treat that nation? Single out the militarists and pacifists? Go into the workings of it, separate out the constituent elements? You cannot. Every member of that country is a member of the team, must take the good with the bad, must pay the debts contracted by the government. *It cannot be a nation otherwise.*

This from your point of view. And from the point of view of the workings of justice it happens to be no less defensible. When the whole of a nation reaps reward or punishment, a rough general justice is executed. If it is only the will of a minority which has brought on catastrophe, and the majority must pay, then it pays for having suffered the will of the minority. Had the German masses foreseen defeat and its consequences, Germany would never have gone to war, militarist minority or none. The masses which obeyed their masters, readily or sullenly, must pay for the obedience which gave their masters strength. . . . And the same is true of every other nation which is guilty.

All extenuation is irrelevant. How shall the majority learn that it *must not* acquiesce indolently in the will of the minority? Shall it not suffer the consequences of its indolence? A slow, almost impossible process. But assuredly a just one. For the impotent or corrupt acquiescence of the majority made the minority effective.

But if, on the other hand, a nation suffers for the will of its majority, and the minority suffers with the majority, then very clearly effective justice is being wrought, and just as clearly is the payment supposed to alter the will of the nation.

As long as there are nations and groups these laws must hold. And as soon as these laws collapse nations and groups will cease to be.

It is not meaningless to say, "This nation is parsimonious, this nation is treacherous, this nation is cruel." It is irrelevant to answer, "You must judge by the individual, not by

126

The Reckoning

the nation." When we say, "Scotchmen are
parsimonious," we simply mean that out of a
thousand Scotchmen a larger number are parsimonious than out of a thousand Englishmen.
A Scotchman whom I do not know has therefore more probability of being parsimonious
than an Englishman whom I do not know. If
therefore I have to choose for generosity between two men, an Englishman and a Scotchman, both of whom I do not know, I would
choose the Englishman. I stand a better
chance of being in the right. Naturally the
entire assumption may be wrong, and that is
another matter, but it is ludicrous to deny that
tendencies or characteristics in nations exist.
Only the shallow demagogue insists that a
thousand Englishmen, a thousand Frenchmen,
a thousand Germans, a thousand Jews, picked
up at random (or ten thousand or a hundred
thousand) would react similarly to the same
stimulus. Assuredly if I have the opportunity
to check up on the individual I will do it. But
if I must take him on trust I shall sensibly
assume him to possess his race characteristics.

You Gentiles

As for you gentiles and us Jews, we have both acted on the assumption that the mass must be treated by a general law. The instinct of the gentile is to distrust the Jew, of the Jew to distrust the gentile. We only make exceptions. There is nothing inconsistent in the anti-Semite who says: "Some of my best friends are Jews."

I say, therefore, that in the conflict between us you have fought us physically, while our attack on your world has been in the spiritual field. It is the nature of the gentile to fight for his honor, in the nature of the Jew to suffer for his. Whether because we are so inclined by first nature, or whether because we have so become through lack of land and government and army—this is true: you revel in force, we despise it, even where we can and do exert it.

And so, since we have lived among you, you have instinctively appealed to brute force in combating our influence. When the reckoning is drawn up your guilt cries to heaven: whatever have been your relations to each other,

we Jews have at least been the common de-
nominator of your brutality. Compared with
each other, you are gentlemen, warriors, democracies: set side by side with us, you are
bullies and cowards and mobs. In vain do
your quiescent majorities wash their hands;
their quiescence is their effective guilt—I care
not that your minorities struck the blow: I
should not acquit the majority if I could give
judgment and impose punishment.

That you are unable to meet us on the
spiritual level is made evident by the following: We are a disturbing influence in your
life not through our own fault. First: we
are not in your midst by our own will, but
through your action; and second (which is
more to the point): we do not attack you
deliberately. We are unwelcome to you because we are what we are. It is our own
positive way of life which clashes with yours.
Our attack on you is only incidental to the
expression of our way of life. You too have
this field open to you. As surely as we are
a spiritual discomfort to you, you are a spirit-

129

ual discomfort to us: as surely as we attack
you peacefully, so you waste us peacefully
and weaken our numbers. But you do more
than this: you bring the attack down to the
physical plane, where we are defenseless.
You do with us as your animal whims dictate;
you rob us, you slay us, you drive us from
land to land, and while one of you drives us
forth the other shuts the gate in our faces.
From the first day of our contact, since the
first of our communities in exile, you have
made us the sport of your brutality. There
is at least one clear note in gentile world-
history, one consistent theme: the note of our
agony—the theme of your cruelty.

Even from your point of view you have
been guilty. On our side at least the fighting
has been clean; we have not misrepresented
you. On your side the fighting has been dirty.
From the dawn of civilization you have lied
about us; you have accused us of murder-
ing children that we might use their blood
for ritual purposes; you have accused us of

130

poisoning wells; you have accused us of precipitating wars (you! and war is the breath
of your nostrils!); and you accuse us to-day
of fomenting a world-wide conspiracy to seize
the government of the world. Do not answer
us that a minority does this. Does it matter
to us that a minority of America preaches in
the Klan virtual disfranchisement of the Jew,
that a minority in Germany preaches death
to the Jew, that a minority in Poland slew
hundreds of us? I ask an accounting of you
as you ask it of one another: as the allies ask
it from Germany, as Germany asked it from
France—from you as a whole. For this
minority which spreads these lies there is a
complacent majority which tolerates or ac-
cepts them. And it is because, in your oppo-
sition to our way of life, you stoop to such
lies that your masses respond with physical
force. I care not how ignorant a Jew is: you
will not get him to believe of one of you such
foul untruths as millions of you believe of
us; yet we have more cogent reason for hat-

ing you. And as I hold you all responsible for these lies, so I hold you all responsible for the cruelties in which they issue.

And I know that soon enough these crimson sluices will be opened again, and we shall bleed from a thousand wounds as we have bled before. In the Ukraine, or in Russia, in Poland or in Germany—and who knows when the same will not come to pass in England, in America, in France? What guarantee have we beyond the guarantee of public opinion? And from a public opinion which tolerates the slaughter of hundreds of negroes, how far to the public opinion which will condone the slaughter of Jews? Let a spark but carry far enough, down into the recesses of your animal natures. How you gloated among the Allies over stories of Germans blown to pieces, cut to pieces; and in the Central Powers over stories of Englishmen, Frenchmen done to death. Your comic journals made merry over them. (A good joke from *Life:* An Englishman, shaking his head, says, "Molly, I don't think this 'ere bayonet'll

The Reckoning

go through more'n two Germans at a time.")
Your women applauded them, your children
screamed for blood: democracy vied in bes-
tiality with aristocracy and royalty. How
shall we trust you?

If we are willing to forget the past, is not
your past your present? Is not the blood
libel alive to-day? And its companion viper,
"the Elders of Zion"? Will poison work
forever in the blood and never break out?
Did not hundreds of thousands of Englishmen, Frenchmen, Germans, Americans, read
these legends without protesting, without
seeking to punish the libelers? Do we not
know how easily your morality fits your
mood? "Kill the Jews, the Christ-killers,"
does indeed ring strange these days. But
does "a damn good dose of lead for the Jewish Bolsheviks" sound very remote?

And if, arguing from the individual to the
mass, your Klans and your Awakening Magyars, your Chestertons and your Daudets
shall call us Jews sharks and swindlers, shall
we not answer with better warrant, by the

133

millions of our murdered, by the Inquisition
and the Crusades, by the smoking ruins of
the Ukraine and the swinging body of Leo
Frank: Dastards, murderers, and thieves!

VIII

But as Moderns

"Let us have done with recollections and recriminations," you say. "You have spoken hitherto of conditions which are vanishing: of orthodox Jews mostly, of old customs and emotions which are dying out. You yourself are not an orthodox Jew; nor are we medieval Christians. We see the Jew gradually modernizing. He becomes more like us—more difficult to recognize as a Jew. Granting there are occasional relapses, we are still moving toward real tolerance. The present age is not like any age before it, and the modern Jew is not like any Jew before him. You have lasted two thousand years in exile—you will not last for ever. All those ceremonials of yours are breaking down: your discipline, your defensive mechanisms. At least in America, England, France, Germany,

135

You Gentiles

Russia you are changing, becoming like us, taking your share in all our activities, sports, civic duties, achievements, arts. You have spoken hitherto in the terms of a world which is fitfully dissolving. You have ignored the liberal Jews, the radical Jews, the modernized Jews, the agnostic Jews, now becoming the dominant element in Jewry, and approaching us, mingling with us, solving the problem without deliberate effort.

"Do not your own radicals renounce their Jewish connections? Will not your modernized Jews be the first to denounce the thesis of this book?"

I have already said, anticipating this objection, that there is the same difference between the Jewish atheist and the gentile atheist as between the orthodox Jew and the believing gentile: I have said or implied that the religion itself is but practical expression of the difference between us, not the cause of it. It is true that the expression of a view serves to strengthen it, as the exercise of a faculty serves to develop it. But expression does not create a view nor exercise a faculty. Even conscious' adherence to the Jewish people is but partial expression of our Jewishness: it was not the conscious desire to remain a people which gave us the will to endure: it was our unavoidable commonalty of feeling which made us and continued us a people.

Repudiation of the Jewish religion or even of Jewish racial affiliation does not alter the Jew. Some of us Jews may delude ourselves as some of you gentiles do. But in effect modernization seems to have done nothing to decrease the friction between us. The dislike continues: and though your masses may not know why they dislike us, there must be a sufficient reason: it is Germany, the mother of the modernized Jew, that gave birth, with him, to modern anti-Semitism. Where the old ostensible reasons for disliking the Jew collapsed, new ones, more self-conscious, were substituted. When modernization removed the old, superstitious form of expression, the professor replaced the priest, science religion.

137

You Gentiles

We are disliked on "scientific" grounds, as we were disliked on "religious." But both the "scientific" and the "religious" reasons were rationalizations. The true reasons underlay these analyses.

Nor can the revulsion of the war, with its release of primitive instincts, be blamed for this. German anti-Semitism antedates the war. The Higher Anti-Semitism has nothing to do with either conscious religion or localizations, like patriotism. It is true modern anti-Semitism. It is the old dislike of the Jew transvaluated into modern terminology, *and it has been evoked by the appearance of that new phenomenon, the Westernized Jew.*

For many Jews were fooled by appearances. They took the word of the gentile literally. The gentile said: "We dislike you because you are different from us in religion and in usages; you are separate; you are old-fashioned." And the Jew, believing these charges to mean what they say, abandoned his customs and his usages: took to baptism;

138

became, externally, similar to the gentile, thinking thus to evade the issue. It failed. For no sooner had he made this change in himself than the gentile shifted ground, went from the religious to the ethnic.

What happened in Germany is happening elsewhere. As fast as the Jew modernizes, so fast does dislike of him adapt itself to the new situation and find a new excuse. Where the Jew is disliked it is the modern Jew who is disliked equally with the old-fashioned. The Klan, the Consul, the Dearborn Independent, the Dwa Grosse, the Action Française no longer preach the modernization of the Jew as a solution of the Jew problem. No Jew, however modern, or radical, is acceptable to the anti-Semite. It is now a *racial* question.

But you still have an answer. You say: "These new forms of anti-Semitism are hangovers: we have had anti-Semitism with us for a long time. It is hard to get rid of. The effects linger long after the cause disappears. But in time . . ."

You Gentiles

This I deny, for I am convinced that the modernized Jew, as long as he retains the quality of the Jewish people, that is, as long as he inherits predominantly 'Jewish characteristics, is as objectionable to you as the orthodox Jew was to your fathers—and for the same basic reasons. The effort of the Jews to enter your modern life, to become part of it, has been essentially ineffective: by which I mean that though hundreds of thousands of us have taken on your garb, speak like you, look like you, share your countries, institutions, games, do all we can to avoid friction, yet we fail to offer in cross section the same significance as any cross section of hundreds of thousands of you. Our ability to imitate extends only to inessentials, appearances, surface desires and ambitions. We fail to be gentiles.

The modernized Jew still stands apart from the modern gentile world, and his effective contribution to its life is as disastrously different as if he still put on the phylacteries every morning. The old racial seriousness, somberness, still persists. In a hundred years of modernity we, an able race, have given little more than mediocrity to your way of life. Our best work has been the old, true work of our people—fundamental and serious examination of the problems of man's relation to God and humanity. In the arts we have been second-rate, third-rate. While in moral effort we have exceeded any living race and have produced an overwhelming number of revolutionaries and socialists and iconoclasts of the true prophetic type, we have, in science, belles-lettres and the plastic arts been a thoroughly minor people. And even if in these last fields we have done comparatively well for our numbers (which I doubt), our preponderant contribution of fundamental moral effort still makes modern Jewry a secularized replica of old religious Jewry.

The astonishing thing is that this took place despite desperate conscious efforts on our part to become like you. We joined your armies and fought in them beyond our numbers: yet Jewish pacifism and Jewish pacifists gave the tone to the world's pacifism. We have joined your capitalistic world in deliberate emulation and rivalry: yet Jewish socialism and Jewish socialists are the banner bearers of the world's "armies of liberation." Three or four million modernized Jews, a ludicrously small number, have given to the world's iconoclastic force its chief impetus and by far its largest individual contribution. America and England put together, with their almost two hundred millions, have not played that rôle in world iconoclasm which a handful of Jews have played. Had we produced as vigorously in art and science we should have flooded the art galleries and the libraries. But in these we have shown no special aptitude: we may have done as well for our numbers as England, as France or Germany— though even this I doubt. But it cannot compare with our rôle as moralists and prophets.

We modern Jews of the Western world are in this fundamentally different from you. The occasional in you (revolution against the

142

But as Moderns

Game) is the dominant in us. Your instinct
is truer than you know. The dislike of your
modern world for the modern Jew is as relevant as the dislike of your old world for the
orthodox Jew.

IX

We, the Destroyers

IF anything, you must learn (and are learning) to dislike and fear the modern and "assimilated" Jew more than you did the old Jew, for he is more dangerous to you. At least the old Jew kept apart from you, was easily recognizable as an individual, as the bearer of the dreaded Jewish world-idea: you were afraid of him and loathed him. But to a large extent he was insulated. But as the Jew assimilates, acquires your languages, cultivates a certain intimacy, penetrates into your life, begins to handle your instruments, you are aware that his nature, once confined safely to his own life, now threatens yours. You are aware of a new and more than disconcerting character at work in the world you have built and are building up, a char-

144

acter which crosses your intentions and thwarts your personality.

The Jew, whose lack of contact with your world had made him ineffective, becomes effective. The vial is uncorked, the genius is out. His enmity to your way of life was tacit before. To-day it is manifest and active. He cannot help himself: he cannot be different from himself: no more can you. It is futile to tell him: "Hands off!" He is not his own master, but the servant of his life-will.

For when he brings into your world his passionately earnest, sinisterly earnest righteousness, absolute righteousness, and, speaking in your languages and through your institutions, scatters distrust of yourselves through the most sensitive of you, he is working against your spirit. You gentiles do not seek or need or understand social justice as an ultimate ideal. This is not your nature. Your world must so be fashioned as to give you the maximum of play, adventure, laughter, animal-lyricism. Your institutions frame

145

themselves to this end: your countries and ideals flourish most gloriously when they serve this end most freely. All ideas of social justice must be subservient to this consideration: the Game first—then ultimate justice only as it can serve the Game.

I do not believe that we Jews are powerful enough to threaten your way of life seriously. We are only powerful enough to irritate, to disturb your conscience, and to break here and there the rhythmic rush of your ideas. We irritate you as a sardonic and humorless adult irritates young people by laughing at their play. For the real irritation lies in the fact that to our queries regarding your life there is no answer on our level: as to yours regarding our life there is no answer on yours.

We Jews are accused of being destroyers: whatever you put up, we tear down. It is true only in a relative sense. We are not iconoclasts deliberately: we are not enemies of your institutions simply because of the dislike between us. We are a homeless mass seeking satisfaction for our constructive in-

146

stincts. And in your institutions we cannot find satisfaction; they are the play institutions of the splendid children of man—and not of man himself. We try to adapt your institutions to our needs, because while we live we must have expression; and trying to rebuild them for our needs, we unbuild them for yours.

Because your chief institution is the social structure itself, it is in this that we are most manifestly destroyers. We take part in the economic struggle for existence: this necessity we share with you. But our free spiritual energies point away from this struggle, for, unlike you, we have no pleasure in it. You gentiles fight because you like to fight; we fight because we have to—and in order to win. It is not in a spirit of hypocrisy that you have turned your business world into a sporting arena, with joyous flourishes, slogans, pretenses. It is not in a spirit of hypocrisy that you talk of playing the Game while you cut each other's throats in the markets. You mean it. Your advertising-propaganda

147

books, with their sentimental appeals, are not lies; they are the true evidence of your spirit. It is only when we Jews, too, use these methods that there is hypocrisy. For we see starkly through your life-illusions: yet we are forced to use them in self-defense. But our inmost longings turn from this fierce and clamorously happy struggle: while your inmost longings are part of it. You give your best to it, yourselves, your souls. We give only our cleverness to it. This is why, in spite of the popular delusion to the contrary, there are hardly any Jews among the world's wealthiest men. The greatest financial institutions, as well as the world's greatest businesses, are almost exclusively non-Jewish.

Dislike of the Jew in business springs from the feeling that we regard all your play-conventions with amusement—or even contempt. Our abominable seriousness breaks jarringly into your life-mood. But you feel our disruptive difference most keenly, most resentfully, in our deliberate efforts to change your social system. We dream of a world of utter

148

justice and God-spirit, a world which would
be barren for you, devoid of all nourishment,
bleak, unfriendly, unsympathetic. You do
not want such a world: you are unapt for it.
Seen in the dazzling lights of your desires
and needs our ideal is repellently morose.

We do wrong to thrust these ideals upon
you, who are not for justice or peace, but for
play-living. But we cannot help ourselves:
any more than you can help resenting our
interference. While we live we must give utterance to our spirit. The most insistent effort on our part will fail to change our nature.

Not that you are untouched by poverty,
by human degradation: not that you do not
wish at times that these unhappy things could
be destroyed. But this is not in the direct
line of march of your life. If social injustice
were removed together with the Game, you
would unquestionably recall both. Life before everything, freedom, joy, adventure.

I talk here of the modern, and not of the
orthodox Jew. I talk of the Jew as alien
as you to the forms of our orthodox and con-

sciously Jewish life: this is the Jew who forms the backbone both of audience and contributor to your radical and revolutionary organs, the Jew who is the precipitating center of your spasmodic and inconsistent efforts for justice. This man, in your midst, is not to be recognized, on the surface, as a Jew. He himself repudiates—and in all sincerity—his Jewish affiliations. He is a citizen of the world; he is a son of humanity; the progress of all humankind, and not of any single group of it, is in his particular care.

It is to this Jew that liberals among you will point to refute my thesis. And it is precisely this Jew who best illustrates its truth. The unbelieving and radical Jew is as different from the radical gentile as the orthodox Jew from the reactionary gentile. The cosmopolitanism of the radical Jew springs from his feeling (shared by the orthodox Jew) that there is no difference between gentile and gentile. You are all pretty much alike: then why this fussing and fretting and fighting? The Jew is *not* a cosmopolitan in your sense.

150

We, the Destroyers

He is not one who feels keenly the difference between national and nation, and overrides it. For him, as for the orthodox Jew, a single temper runs through all of you, whatever your national divisions. The radical Jew (like the orthodox Jew) is a cosmopolitan in a sense which must be irritating to you: for he does not even understand why you make such a fuss about that most obvious of facts —that you are all alike. The Jew is altogether too much of a cosmopolitan—even for your internationalists.

Nor, in the handful of you who, against the desires and instincts of the mass of you, proclaim social justice as the life aim, is the Jew any more truly at home, at one with his milieu, than the old-time Jew in his world. Our very radicalism is of a different temper. Our spur is a natural instinct. We do not have to uproot something in ourselves to become "radicals," dreamers of social justice. We are this by instinct: we do not see it as something revolutionary at all. It is tacit with us. But with you it is an effort and

a wrench. Your very ancestry cries out
against it in your blood. . . . And you become silly and enthusiastic about it, with
flag-waving, and shouting, and battle-hymns,
and all the regular game-psychology proper
to your world and way of life. Even of this
you make a play.

But such as these radical and international
movements are, the modern Jew (the best and
most thoughtful modern Jew, that is) is
nearer to them than to anything else in your
world. He is the only true socialist and cosmopolitan—but in such a true and tacit sense
that he is completely distinguished from all
of you. It is one of many vital paradoxes—
a thing illogical and yet true to life. It is
our very cosmopolitanism that gives us our
national character. Because we are the only
ones who are cosmopolitan by instinct rather
than by argument we remain forever ourselves.

In everything we are destroyers—even in
the instruments of destruction to which we
turn for relief. The very socialism and inter-

152

nationalism through which our choked spirit
seeks utterance, which seem to threaten your
way of life, are alien to our spirit's demands
and needs. Your socialists and internationalists are not serious. The charm of these
movements, the attraction, such as it is, which
they exercise, is only in their struggle: it is
the fight which draws your gentile radicals.
And indeed, it is only as long as there is an
element of adventure in being a radical that
the radical movement retains any individuality. And it is only in the fierce period of
early combat that you welcome us Jews—as
allies. You are deluded in this—so are we.
You go into the movement boldly, adventur-
ously; we, darkly, tacitly. You make it a
game; we do it because we cannot help ourselves. And sure enough, in the end, the
split comes again. The liberal and the radical are as apt to dislike the Jew as the reactionaries are. The liberal and the radical
do not use the weapons of the reactionaries:
but the dislike is there, finds expression in
anti-Semitic socialist and workers' move-

ments and in the almost involuntary contempt which springs to the lips of countless intellectuals.

Philosophies do not remold natures. What your radicals want is another form of the Game, with other rules. Their discontent joins hands with Jewish discontent. But it is not the same kind of discontent. A little distance down the road the ways part for ever. The Jewish radical will turn from your social movement: he will discover his mistake. He will discover that nothing can bridge the gulf between you and us. He will discover that the spiritual satisfaction which he thought he would find in social revolution is not to be purchased from you. I believe the movement has already started, the gradual secession of the Jewish radicals, their realization that your radicalism is of the same essential stuff as your conservatism. The disillusionment has set in.

A century of partial tolerance gave us Jews access to your world. In that period the great attempt was made, by advance guards of rec-

154

onciliation, to bring our two worlds together. It was a century of failure. Our Jewish radicals are beginning to understand it dimly.

We Jews, we, the destroyers, will remain the destroyers for ever. *Nothing* that you will do will meet our needs and demands. We will for ever destroy because we need a world of our own, a God-world, which it is not in your nature to build. Beyond all temporary alliances with this or that faction lies the ultimate split in nature and destiny, the enmity between the Game and God. But those of us who fail to understand that truth will always be found in alliance with your rebellious factions, until disillusionment comes. The wretched fate which scattered us through your midst has thrust this unwelcome rôle upon us.

X

The Games of Science

ILLUSIONS change the instruments of their expression—but they remain the same illusions. Religions change their gods, but remain the same religions. The atheist gentile has made Science his god, but it has not changed his religion.

"In the scientific field," the atheist gentile tells me, "we will find world unity. In science there is no room for the subconscious, and it is the subconscious which dictates the eternal enmities. Place your relations on a conscious basis, and you may have differences to be adjusted—but not enmities.

"The solution of the Jewish-gentile problem, as of every instinct problem, lies in the pursuit of Truth through science. All other problems are not really problems, but purely technical matters, to be settled by the application of mathematics. And as we learn to make this distinction between instinct-problem and technical task, the greater is the discredit into which the former falls, the clearer is the attention which we bring to the latter. The greatest contribution of science to human advance has been the opening of paths to our free intelligence, so that the unconscious and subconscious mind, with its inheritance of the beast, might fall into desuetude. The truth alone will save us—and in science is truth."

I do not wish to go into an examination of the nature of truth; I do not wish to question the validity of scientific truths. I am ready to admit that scientific truths are truths in the accepted sense of this word. Or, if there are mistakes, if this or that scientific theory is wrong, I will not argue that therefore the scientific method is wrong, or that science itself does not go nearest to the truth. My contention is that science, the examination of facts in literal terms, is quite irrelevant to the spiritual problems of man. Science is accurate, but its accuracy is pointless for spiritual purposes. The truths which are unveiled by the scientific method, and which it is the special aptness of this method to unveil, do not matter to anybody.

Science teaches us that the earth goes around the sun, rather than the sun round the earth. Does it really matter which is the case? Science teaches us that the occasional retrogression effect in the observed motion of the planets is not due to "cycle in epicycle, orb in orb," but to changes of perspective produced along the plane of the ecliptic during the revolutions of the planets round the sun. Well, what of it? It has revealed the fact that certain diseases are due to the action of minute parasites; that there is a marvelous structural parallel between man and the beasts; that forms of energy are interchangeable; that the earth is extremely old; that there were other forms of life on the planet before us; that we are merely a point in space. All this is accurate: but is it of any importance?

I ignore, of course, the obvious advantages

which are supposed to accrue from the application of these facts—"the conquest of nature" as it is bombastically called: though even these advantages are vitiated by our inability to exploit them decently. It is not to these advantages that the scientist alludes when he talks of the spiritual value of science. He means pure science: the perception of these truths for their own sake or, more accurately, for the sake of the change which they produce in our attitude toward life, the universe, each other.

But science and revelation of scientific truths have no effect on our attitude toward life, the universe and each other. The mood of the mind of man, the temper of his outlook, his essential nature—this totality of spiritual reaction—has nothing to do with the additional number of facts which science reveals. It would not alter the effective mood of civilized man if it happened that light were revealed as the radiation of corpuscles rather than as waves in the ether, whatever that may mean. There may be eighty-eight elements, or eight hundred and eighty: the atom may be a kind of solar system, or it may be a figure of speech: life may be the function of a complicated molecular structure or it may be an illusion: whichever should turn out to be "true," we should remain the same: our only concern is with the exploitation of these things for physical advantages, and as far as that is concerned it does not matter whether we have the truth or have hit on a method by conventional hypothesis. The Ptolemaic system of astronomy could permit the calculation of eclipses as accurately as the Copernican. "Cycle in epicycle, orb in orb" works as effectively, if the figures are closely enough watched, as ellipses with the sun at one of the foci.

For science is a game, a particular systematization, which might well be any other systematization. Indeed, despite the prodigious number of facts which science has unveiled, no new type of spiritual outlook has been evolved. Is the general consciousness or self-consciousness of the modern materialist different in effect from that of the civilized Stoic of more than two thousand years ago? If you substitute "stress in the ether" for the Pneuma, if you substitute the laws of gravitation, or some electro-magnetic formula for each other or for "tension," will that alter your response to the universe?

Science is so far a game, indeed, that, self-confessedly, it deals with symbols only. These are pure abstractions—the ion, X^n, the theory of relativity. We juggle with figures, with symbols, with arrangements; the *things* or *truths* or *facts* which are supposedly represented are utterly beyond our apprehension. To take the simplest illustration: the sun is ninety-two million miles from the earth, the moon a quarter of a million miles. Neither of these distances means anything to any human being: a million, or ten million, or a thousand billion—we have no spiritual reaction to any of these figures. They are symbols or counters in the game; in themselves intelligible to no one.

Or to take the most significant of new sci-

entific truths—the theory of relativity. Its
application is only to the game or system.
No man himself reacts to its implications.
He uses in it the laboratory, in the observa-
tory. He cannot bring it out. He cannot
even lift it off the paper. Indeed, such a
revolution was wrought in our "conception of
the universe" by the exposition of the theory
of relativity that, if scientific truths had any
spiritual significance, there should have been
a religious revolution in its wake. Since the
dawn of science we have been blind to a tremendous and fundamental truth, an all-inclu-
sive and inescapable truth—namely, that the
motion of light rules all our measurements
of time and space and mass—that the length
of a line or of a period of time is nothing but
a function of varying values. A terrific and
sublime discovery, one might say. Yet not
only does it fail to make a particle of difference to the spiritual attitude of scientists toward the universe: they cannot even the-
oretically integrate it with a spiritual system.

All the effective "spiritual" value of the

162

theory of relativity is: "Things are not what they seem." To this suspicion—which is a basic spiritual reaction of man to the universe—the theory of relativity adds nothing. At most the theory of relativity is an additional but superfluous illustration.

But I shall be told by the scientist: "It is not any individual scientific revelation which matters. What matters is the scientific outlook, as such, the conception of the universe as an ordered and harmonious process: the elimination of the providential and accidental: the final and decisive removal of the thaumaturgical. Science means neither the theory of evolution, nor the discovery of the bacillus, nor the theory of relativity. Science means the cancellation of the inherited instinct errors. In brief, science is the substitution of reason for superstition."

But even at that variation I contend that "scientific" pursuit of truth has given nothing to our knowledge of the ultimate secret of things. What the scientist would call the "scientific outlook"—in accordance with the

above definition—has nothing to do with
"scientific study of phenomena." Men are
by nature unthaumaturgical or thaumaturgical in their reaction to the universe. Science
(in its modern sense) does not make them
unthaumaturgical. It is one of the basic
qualities of human thought—this particular
variety of outlook on the universe. I say
it existed before the advent of what we de-
note under the restricted term of science. I
say it would exist just as strongly in these
types of men though not a single discovery
had been added to human knowledge of phenomena since the time of Aristotle. I say
that though science should add a million
startling new revelations to its old ones, it
would not increase or decrease the number
of men who have the "unthaumaturgical"
outlook.

I referred to the Stoics and said that Stoi-
cism contained as unthaumaturgical an outlook as any that "modern science" claims to
have inspired. But even if this were not true
I should not change my opinion, for life at

first hand taught me this view, and what I know of history I used only as an illustration. Life at first hand has taught me that knowledge of science has nothing to do with the superstitious or unsuperstitious, with the thamaturgical or unthaumaturgical, with idealism or materialism. I have known thoroughly "ignorant" men who see life quite rationally, apparently untroubled by unconscious impulses: men who have "the scientific outlook" without knowing or needing science. I have known thoroughly scientific men who are profoundly thaumaturgical, who are saturated with the spirit of superstition.

It is not the knowledge of facts which changes the man. A man may believe in ghosts and yet not be superstitious—he may merely be mistaken. Another man may believe neither in ghosts nor in an anthropomorphic God and yet be essentially of the superstitious type.

It is not even a question of sophistication. I have known simple and primitive peasants, quite illiterate, who were as clearly rationalist

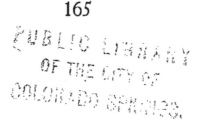

and scientific in outlook as any professor inspired by a complete knowledge of the revealed mechanics of the world. I have known cultured city dwellers, rotten with sophistication, whose surface cynicism could not hide their subjection to the terror of invisible, unrevealable possibilities.

Scientific genius is only the genius of the ingenious. Men who by their nature are materialists spend their energies in building intensely ingenious schemata wherein the known facts of life constitute the sole material. But these ingenious schemata do not alter their nature with their shape or with the quantity of their material. The mechanics of the universe might be thus or thus; things might work in this way or in that way; it might be one formula or another formula. But the spirit of the thing is the same. For hundreds of years capable minds have searched, constructed, reconciled. Their knowledge of the mechanism is infinitely greater that any man's knowledge a thousand years ago. Yet men who know as little of these mechanics as was known a thousand years ago have come to the same conclusion regarding the nature of the universe.

There is in science a certain *naïveté:* the belief that facts differ in their nature; the belief that a fact which it is more difficult to unearth is therefore profounder than a fact which is obvious; the belief that a microbe, because it needs a microscope to reveal it, touches truth more deeply than the flea, which can be seen with the naked eye: yet a fact is not more valuable for being difficult of access, any more than a thought is more profound by having been made obscure.

In the end it comes to this: science, which is the accumulation of literal fact, hopes that the accumulation of facts will reveal the nature of fact. Science seems to believe (if I may use these rather clumsy locutions) that some facts are of a different order from other facts, going nearer to the sources of the nature of things. This is untrue. All facts are on the same plane. Facts are not explanatory, but expository, and what they ex-

167

pose is of the same nature or material as that which we know without science. To expect facts to reveal the nature of facts is to expect the microscope to reveal the nature of the microscope. You *can* examine one microscope by means of another: but its nature, or secret, is not accessible to this mode of examination. It is of a different order. The chain of facts is everywhere uniform. When you know one inch of this chain, you have learned as much as you can learn from a mile. If the chain of causes and effects, fact related to fact, is infinitely long, any length of it is equally insignificant. A thousand years is not nearer to eternity than a moment of time.

There is, indeed, a certain vulgarity in the appeal to quantity; it is the democratic vulgarity, the belief that one million mediocre people have more spiritual significance than one mediocrity; that size affects quality; that one thousand new facts mean more than a hundred old facts—there is in all this even the vulgarity of provincialism and cockney fashionableness, the belief that the latest is the best.

.. But vulgarity is most patent in the common assertion, that science is of spiritual value because it reveals the wonders of the universe. So marvelous a structure, they say, rouses our astonishment and our reverence—"the glory of God's house" and "the infinite wisdom of his ways," "science leads to religion because it teaches us both our own insignificance and the amazing cleverness of creation."

I hold this view to be patently vulgar because it is an appeal to headlines: recourse to the stimuli of the advertiser for the benefit of a stupid and jaded public. The thinking man needs no scientist to teach him the wonder of creation: he needs neither a telescope nor a microscope in order to see God; nor do formulæ teach him the nature of God. Life itself, being, the staggering wonder of mere existence, fills completely, crams beyond all possibility of addition, the faculty of astonishment and bewilderment in the sensitive

man. Those to whom existence has become
commonplace by familiarity—or who have
never been smitten prostrate by the riddle of
existence—need a crescendo succession of
"shockers" to touch their brutish minds.
They didn't know the marvel of the universe
until they learned of electricity; but now that
electricity is as commonplace as sunlight, they
need a theory of relativity; and when that is
played out as an advertising stunt for the
ingenuity of the Almighty, they will need
something else.

Such vulgarity in scientists is not a whit
different from the vulgarity of city mobs,
which crow with astonishment when first they
see an electric light, but afterwards smile
pityingly at those who manifest astonishment. The man of the mass mistakes impudent familiarity for understanding. Because
he uses the electric car, the telephone and the
telegraph every day he imagines that he is
wiser than the barbarian who has never known
of them. If at all, he is less wise, being too
impudent to know his own ignorance. The

170

fool that saith in his heart there is no God is the city fool to whom nothing is wonderful any more: and those who do not know wonder do not know God.

Is it not significant that the greatest human cry of wonder—the Bible—was the utterance of men who knew nothing concerning the pleiseiosaurus, the amœba, the nebula of Orion, Mendeleyeff's tables, Bode's law, the theory of quanta? In them the marvel of existence shocked like a clash of cymbals: the echoes of that first, fresh amazement still put to shame the sophisticated stammering of this wise age. Have all the revelations of science brought just a single utterance like that of Job? Though a man should master all the ingenuities of science, though he should double and treble them, though he should know all the workings of his own body and of the stellar systems, though earth's past and future, the past and future of all life, should lie open before him, can he say or feel more than this?

Can science even add anything to skepti-

171

cism and doubt? Shall he who suspects that
all life is a phantasm, perception itself the
shadow of a shadow, and our very whispers
to ourselves the ten-times-tampered-with instruments of things which are not ourselves:
shall he that suspects that between himself
and himself, himself-speaking and himself-
listening, himself-thinking and himself-
thought-of, there looms, world without end,
system within system, aberration within aberration: shall such a one be rendered more
doubtful because the sky is *not* an inverted
bowl above our heads, because disease is carried not by demons but by invisible fleas?
If the whole is insecure, does the double in-
security of a part make any difference? If
all is illusory, does it matter that there were
particular little illusions within the general
illusion? If we suspect the very instrument
of our perception, if we doubt our senses and
our thoughts, if we doubt our very doubts,
and in the end, from a frantic hunting of pro-
tean shadows, relapse into utter silence and
impotence—what additional impotence is to

The Games of Science

be derived from the correction of unscientific errors?

The world's wonder, the world's doubt, the terror and illusion of life—these things lie patent to the naked eye. Life at first hand teaches everything. The blind cannot see even through a microscope.

What, then, is science, and wherein lies its lure? Why are men drawn to its service, why do the best and ablest give up their lives to its pursuit?

Science, which can be of no ultimate value in bringing us nearer to the roots of life, to Godhead and its secrecies; science is a Game, a convention. The charm of science is the charm of gentile life. The ultimate does not matter: within the system there is the lyric grace of rhythm and harmony.

The scientific development of your Western world is an inevitable consequence of your nature. It is inevitable that you should worship science, because your very skepticism is the substitution of one set of illusions for another, the adoption of one set of conventions in place of another. You are bound to find "spiritual value" in science because you do not want ultimate spiritual value—only the spiritual value of immediate lyric enjoyment. You who worship gods instead of God must naturally worship science. Science is merely idol-worship: for eikons instruments, for incantations formulæ: the palpable, the material, the enjoyable. Science is not a serious pursuit: your grave professors of chemistry, astronomy, physics, your Nobel prize-winners are but bald or bearded schoolboys playing mental football for their own delight and the delight of spectators.

Science, then, is an art, though its technique is of so peculiar a nature as to divide it from all the other arts: but we most easily recognize it as an art because the true scientist takes an artistic delight in science.

And because your science is not serious, we Jews have never achieved in it any peculiar preëminence. We have our few exceptions: we can master as well as you the system and the scheme, but we lack the spiritual urge, the driving joy, the illusion that this is the all in all.

We know nothing of science for science's sake—as we know nothing of art for art's sake. We only know of art for God's sake. If there is art or beauty in our supreme production, the Bible, it is not because we sought either. The type of the artist is alien to us, and just as alien is the delight of the artist. The artist is one who seeks beauty, goes out of his way to find her. But the Hebrew prophet, who wrought so beautifully, did not go out of his way to find God. God pursued him and caught him; hunted him out and tortured him so that he cried out. Until this day we have no artists in your sense: such art as we have created has been the by-product of a fierce moral purpose.

Art and science—this is your gentile world, a lovely and ingenious world. Kaleidoscopic, graceful, bewilderingly seductive, a world, at its best, of lovely apparitions, banners, struggles, triumphs, gallantries, noble gestures and conventions. But not our world, not for us

175

Jews. For such Field-of-the-Cloth-of-Gold
delights we lack imagination and inventiveness. We are not touched with this vigor of
productive playfulness. Under duress we
take part in the ringing mêlée, and give an
indifferently good account of ourselves. But
we have not the heart for this world of yours.

XI

The Masses

It would be absurd to pretend that the Jewish masses are distinguished from your masses by a conscious appreciation of the difference I have described. Indeed, very few even of the thinking Jews understand the nature of the problem. It is certain that the Westernized masses of Jews are doing their best to minimize, or to ignore, the difference between Jew and gentile: they and their leaders assert, frequently and vehemently, that there is no difference. Jew and gentile are alike except in their opinions regarding certain very simple "matters of faith."

You, too, will assert: "Even if we grant this distinction between gentile and Jewish genius, are we to understand that it permeates the masses, that the strain of seriousness is to be found in your hundreds of thousands of

You Gentiles

Westernized workers, lawyers, salesmen, merchants, manufacturers, contrasting with a corresponding levity or lack of seriousness in the same classes among us? It is incredible. The same language, the same occupations, the same sports, the same pursuits are common to both of us. Let any intelligent man live first for ten years among middle-class gentile families and then change his milieu completely and pass into the environment of middle-class, assimilated Jewish families. What will there be to give him the impression of another world? Will he not find the same amusements, the same ambitions, the same morality, the same taboos, the same abilities and the same stupidities? Do not the Jewish and gentile middle-class families admire the same heroes, vote for the same politicians, read the same newspapers and magazines, frequent the same theaters, weep over the same movies, laugh at the same comic strips?"

But the question cannot be put so simply. This world is yours, and you are the ones who set the standards. You are the ones who supply the material for the reactions. And when we Jews want to become part of your world, enjoy its privileges and pleasures, we must accept your standards, speak, as it were, the same language. But just as a word can never mean quite the same thing to two persons, so a common expression does not mean the same emotion.

The fact is that as long as Jews retain their identity there is the same tension between your middle classes and ours as between your genius and ours. Our middle classes, even when thoroughly modernized, retain a certain individuality which is repugnant to you. And though, if forced to a yes-or-no answer to the question above enunciated, I should have to answer: "Yes, there is a difference, difficult to describe, but felt and resented none the less."

Our modernized Jews have done their best to take up your life and become part of it, but despite outward appearances they have failed. There is, first of all, too eager and intense a desire to be gentile. What you do

179

tacitly, and by the grace of God, we do deliberately and in the gracelessness of ambition. You grew into this new life of yours. We contort ourselves into it. In one or two generations we would achieve what it took you a hundred generations to reach. We take up your life with an anxiousness, a ferocity, which is its own undoing. Whatever in you can be imitated, we do imitate admirably, but though you cannot quite define it, you are aware of a deception. Our patriotisms are hysterical; our sport pursuits are unnaturally eager; our business ambitions artificially passionate. We seek the same apparent ends as you, but not in the same spirit. Would you have us fight and die for country? We'll do it as well as you. Would you have us run fast, box skilfully? We'll do it. Would you have us build up enterprises? We'll do that too. But one thing we cannot do. Do it for the same reason and in the same spirit.

Since you insist, we will measure values with your standards and register the results. But you know, you feel, that the standards

are not ours. We betray ourselves, singly
and in mass. We haven't the manner. And
we haven't the manners—for manners are but
a manner with you.

We Jews are lacking in manners because
manners, as you have evolved them, are a
spirit, a reflex of your play world. Manners
cannot be copied: one must have the aptitude
for this charming triviality. A single note of
insistence spoils it all. And we Jews insist
too much.

And just as Jews are without manners, so
they are without vulgarity. I have observed
that between the vulgar gentile and the so-
called vulgar Jew there is a singular and
dreadful difference. The vulgar type of gentile is not repellent: there is in him an animal grossness which shocks and braces, but
does not horrify: he carries it off by virtue
of a natural brutality and brutishness which
provide a mitigating consistency to his character. But the lowest type of Jew is extraordinarily revolting. There is in him a
suggestion of deliquescent putrefaction. The

181

gentile can be naturally, healthily vulgar. The Jew corrupts into vulgarity—he has not the gift for it. What is vulgarity in the gentile is obscenity in the Jew. I am able to watch, either with amusement or indifference, a vulgar performance on the gentile stage. On the Jewish stage I find it intolerably loathsome. In the company of low and brutish gentiles "let loose" I may not feel at home, but I can be an unmoved spectator. But when Jews try to imitate this behavior I feel my innermost decency outraged. Well-mannered gentile society rejects us. So does vulgar gentile society.

An individual genius cannot be taken as the higher type of the people which produced him: but in the mass there is an inevitable correspondence between the product of the geniuses of a people and the people itself. Studied actuarially, the people finds utterance in the geniuses. There is an undoubted consistency in all the products of the greatest Jewish minds. Whether we take these statistics laterally, through an age, or vertically,

182

through history, we will obtain a similar result. Whether we begin with the Bible and take the sum total of our work down to Karl Marx, or confine ourselves to a single country and generation (America to-day, for instance —with Untermeyer, Lewisohn, Frank, Hecht) we will find the same appeal to fundamentals, the same passionate rejection of your sport world and its sport morality, the same ultimate seriousness, the same inability to be merely playful, merely romantic, merely lyrical.

It is unthinkable that the masses of a people can mean one thing, its geniuses another. Were this so the utterances of great minds would lose all relevance, would become pointless and impotent. If we symbolize a people as a single organism, its geniuses may be likened to an organ of self-consciousness; and the self-consciousness of a man is not an independent function, but the instrument of all of him: all his body and being thinks—through the brain.

That which genius illuminates is the life

from which it springs. The amorphous is crystallized in it: the confused diffusion is brought to a focus, so that the pattern is made clear. Our geniuses, in the midst of your world, are an alien and destructive element, more clearly revealed as such because they are articulate. They are our spokesmen; or, better said, ourselves in utterance. They, like us, being us, cannot join your game. You say, "Because they lack imagination." In a sense it is true. We are unimaginative, as old people are unimaginative in the presence of young people. We neither play with emotions nor with things; we lack romanticists as we lack inventors—because we lack inventiveness.

Even among the masses, where diffusion confuses, an apt instance points to the truth. Among our simple people you do not find the delight in constructive trifles which is one of your characteristics. Your simple people like to build things, fix this and that in the house, play the handy man; they take pleasure in putting up shelves, looking to the plumbing,

184

adding and altering. We are devoid of this kind of craftsman's pleasure; we do what is necessary, only because it is necessary. And as a man, engaged happily in such pleasant, childlike pursuits, resents the chilling indifference of an unsympathetic onlooker, so your world resents our uncalled-for analysis of your acts and occupations. This is your life and you enjoy it. Why do we disturb you with questions concerning ultimate values?

We lack inventiveness. You will say that this springs from our lack of vitality. Men are lyrical because life sings in them; they are inventive because life is restless in them and drives their fingers to activity. I will not argue the cause of the difference, but, lacking inventiveness, we also lack sympathy for it. In your delight you call inventiveness the conquest of nature. But the boast is, to us, a foolish and a childlike boast. The problem with which man is faced cannot be answered by scientific inventions. The conquest of nature does not lie in evolving keener

185

sight, swifter motion, larger strength. This is but magnification, which leaves the element of the problem untouched. Can you conquer, not nature, but the nature of things?

For it is in the nature of things that the bitter problem resides. If science should double the span of human life, will the nature of life and death be altered? Will we not feel as mortal, as insignificant? Will we even be aware of living longer? If science should bridge the planets and the stars, will the new playground be larger than the old to those that live in it? You have found a whole world since the days of the Greeks: they lived on a tiny plot of earth, an ant-hill; and you have a gigantic globe to build on. What difference has it made? What significant conquest have you achieved? Not things but the nature of things baffle us, the dreadful circle, the eternal balance, for every gain a compensating loss, for every new revelation a new deception, for every new extension a loss of intensity.

The nature of things cannot be solved because we partake of that nature. We can never get round ourselves: we can only turn round. Your world spins in a joyous illusion of progress; we, untouched by that illusion, destructive of your mood, stand aside, static, serious. We will be satisfied with nothing but the absolute.

That aloofness speaks clearly or obscurely in our masses as well as in our geniuses. Dealing with objects, instead of with laws, they betray the same unenthusiastic objectivity in their attitude to your world.

And as long as they retain their Jewish identity, they will, despite denial and effort to the contrary, remain the same.

XII

Solution and Dissolution

DOES the situation which I have described
constitute a problem? Or is it merely one
of the insoluble difficulties of life which, being insoluble, should be understood as such
and suffered tacitly? Death is not a problem, being inevitable. Is this struggle between our two worlds as inevitable? Shall
we resign ourselves to the struggle and do
what we can to mitigate its worst effects, or
shall we continue the search for a complete
solution?

The one solution which is generally offered
as complete and satisfactory is, quite apart
from its feasibility, not a solution at all: only
a dissolution. The disappearance of the Jewish people by complete submergence in the
surrounding world would not, in reality, solve
the problem; any more than one solves a

chess problem by burning chess-board and figures. But it would seem to do the next best thing: it would apparently destroy the situation which creates the problem. The problem, without having been solved, would at any rate cease to exist.

And by the dissolution of the Jewish people can be meant only one thing—the disappearance of Jewish identity in individuals or masses, the complete obliteration of Jewish self-consciousness, down to the very name and recollection. When it will be impossible for any man to say of himself, "I am a Jew," or "My father, or grandfather was a Jew" this consummation will have been achieved.

There is only one instrument to this end: free and unrestrained intermarriage. This act or fact alone will count. The mere changing of names, the substitution of religious forms, the so-called "liberalization" and "modernization" of Judaism is ineffective: it is a matter of common observation that there is no inverse ratio between the Westernization of the Jew and anti-Semitism. And this very

189

fact will have to be considered again in its relation to the feasibility of this proposal. If we talk of the submergence of the Jew we must not play with words: words alone cannot submerge the Jew. If there is anything in what I have said you cannot make a gentile of a Jew by arguing with him any more than by lynching him. You can make his children half gentile, his grandchildren only a quarter Jewish—and so on till the balance is perfect.

And this truth seems to have worked in the minds of some Westernizing Jews. Reform Judaism, or modernized Judaism, is the halfway house to baptism: or at least to intermarriage. Its very purpose is such, despite the protestations of Reform Jews. It cannot be anything else, for if the desire is to become "like the world around us," then all barriers must go down, and the real barrier, the conservator of all distinctions, is our practice of endogamy.

One thing is quite certain: a Jew is never baptized for the purpose of becoming a Christian; his purpose is to become a gentile. Yet

190

Solution and Dissolution

obviously you do not make a gentile of a Jew by baptizing him any more than you would make an Aryan of a negro by painting him with ocher. The sole (and sufficient) value in this direction of baptism is the removal of all conscious prohibition against intermarriage.

Of course even baptism is not a necessary preparation. Jews marry gentiles without this preliminary formality. The case is somewhat different here. This is a natural wastage or attrition: individual passion, not policy, is the cause, though the effect is the same—the disappearance of the Jew. And it certainly connotes, even if indirectly, the renunciation first of Judaism and then of Jewish affiliation. A Jew married to a gentile may remain a Jew ostensibly, as he is in fact. His children seldom, if ever, profess Judaism or associate themselves with the Jewish people.

In this case the evasion is even more dishonest than in the first. A man who professes to belong to the Jewish faith and the Jewish people and who nevertheless gives his chil-

191

dren to the gentiles is making the best of
both worlds. He evades the odious name of
renegade which attaches to the baptized Jew
(also salving his conscience) and at the same
time contributes effectively to the dissolution
of the Jewish people. It is well to note that
the Westernized or "Reform" Jew may deplore the practice, but will not exclude such a
man from the Temple. The orthodox Jew
considers such a man lost to Judaism: the
view, whatever its ethics, is clearer and
healthier.

But I want to consider not the accidental,
but the deliberate, or politic. Accidental intermarriage, being accidental and therefore
uncontrollable, is not a policy. Baptism is a
policy: the weakening of Judaism by the removal of its "nationalist" implications, and
by its "modernization," is also a policy—the
same policy, in fact, but more circumspect
and less self-confessed. This policy has as
its objective the solution of the Jewish problem by the dissolution of the Jewish people.

Solution and Dissolution

I will consider later whether this policy can obtain this objective. The question here concerns the objective. Will the "dissolution of Jewish identity" by free and prolonged intermarriage resolve the struggle of the two types? Or will the struggle continue in another form, less obvious but equally uncomfortable? Will the struggle center round isolated individuals, recurrent types? Or will the final product be homogeneous and, in relation to this particular struggle, static?

Both the negative and affirmative answers to this question are unsatisfactory. Suppose, on the one hand, the struggle continues? Suppose the Jewish character persists in strains, breaks out in individual atavisms, long after the Jewish name has perished? The problem will be the same: your world will be confronted with recurrent instances of alien and destructive types, all the more dangerous because they are not isolated in a recognized, repudiated group. Their power of destruction will be the greater because they will

193

work from within. The "Jewish" problem
will have disappeared, but the gentile problem would remain as bitter as ever.

Let us examine the negative answer. Suppose there are no "reversions to type." Suppose the Jew is so completely absorbed as to
be lost beyond possibility of detection in the
surrounding world. Such a consummation, if
possible, calls for one inevitable condition;
that is, the proportionate Judaization of your
world. It is unthinkable that so vivid an element as the Jewish people should be absorbed
into your world without producing an appre-
ciable alteration in its constitution. A world
that has absorbed the Jews will to that extent
be a Jewish world.

And this is precisely the condition which
you refuse to admit. You want no tamper-
ing with your identity; you want to remain
what you are. You have no intention of
meeting us at the point of balance. You do
not want a world tinged with Jewish blood.
You want us to be absorbed in you without
leaving a trace. And with the best intentions

194

Solution and Dissolution

in the world we cannot oblige. We can, in that sense, no more destroy ourselves than we can destroy a single particle of matter.

But I shall show in the following pages that all this talk of dissolution is academic. Even if you should tolerate in prospect both of these alternatives, there are insuperable obstacles which make it highly improbable that you will ever be faced with either.

XIII

The Mechanism of Dissolution

THIS would be an ideal condition, presumably—the merging together of Jew and gentile, for the production of a world neither wholly gentile nor yet dual with Jew and gentile—but composed of both in certain proportions fixed by our numbers and the laws of heredity. That is, at least, the best solution within view, and if we are to be reasonable—on paper at least—it would be the only one to be considered.

But we must remember that this ideal cannot be realized in one generation or in two, or in five. If we were to assume (the assumption is an absurd one) that within this generation the Jewish world could be won over to this point of view, it would still need four or five generations (probably more) to obliterate our identity. At that it would call

196

The Mechanism of Dissolution

for forcible inter-marriage, for even when we cease to believe in endogamy, we will practise it because our affections so incline us. It would have to become a sort of principle— that in the name of the great ideal of a solution of the Jewish problem, the Jew shall be forbidden (morally, at least) to marry among his own. But it is clear that even if intensive propaganda were to break down (it could not, for reasons I shall return to) our prohibitions against inter-marriage, it would have to work progressively. It would take many generations to carry the change successively through all the strongholds of Jewish life. And when we add to the time thus needed the time needed for actual absorption by intermarriage, we are faced with a task for centuries.

But I will deal with ideal conditions. I will deal with a single large group of Jews determined to abandon their identity and to lose themselves and their children in the surrounding gentile world. We know well that their children will not yet be assimilated in the full sense of the word: children of mixed Jewish-gentile percentage still carry the Jewish stigma. The child of a half-Jew and complete gentile is in better plight: and a Jewish great-grandfather is hardly any handicap at all. The third generation, as the saying is, produces the gentleman.

It needs at least these three generations of intermediary stage—probably more. It would be absurd to expect absorption in a single generation: it never happens. There is needed a transition period *and it is this transition period which you gentiles will not tolerate.* Even if you believe (as most of you do) that the best thing that could happen to the Jew would be his complete absorption by inter-marriage, you oppose, tacitly, but not the less obstinately, his steps in that direction. You want us to inter-marry—but *you* don't want to inter-marry. You want us to produce gentile offspring without having taken your sons and daughters as mates.

In other words, you want an end without permitting the means. The prospect of a

198

The Mechanism of Dissolution

Jew-less world is charming indeed, but who will enjoy the actuality? Your grandchildren and great-grandchildren. And who will have to pay the price of the first embarrassing contact, the first difficult intimacy, Jewish sons-and daughters-in-law, Jewish fathers and mothers-in-law? You yourselves. The prospect is too distant, too hypothetical, to exert any influence. It is much too much like the promise of heaven and the threat of hell.

I have alluded more than once to the fact that Westernization of the Jew is nowhere a guarantee against anti-Semitism. Indeed, conscious modern anti-Semitism, the formulated fear of the Jew as the racial bearer of alien and dangerous ideas, is the result of Westernization. Far from encouraging or tolerating our inter-marriage with you, you do not even relish the results of our Westernization or gentilization. It is an amazing and terrifying paradox: you would like us to be absorbed, but you shrink from the process. The inoculation is painful, even revolting. You are uneasy and unhappy when we swarm into your universities, your professions: the nearer we come to you, the more you dislike us. You dislike us because we are different, and when we make efforts to overcome the difference we are forced into a proximity which rouses your inmost resentment. The Ku Klux Klan, the Awakening Magyars, the Consul, no longer warn you against the religious and secluded Jew, the Ghetto and the Talmud. They warn you against the baptizing Jew, against the assimilating Jew, against the inter-marrying Jew. They warn you, indeed, against that part of the Jewish people which is apparently in the process of realization of that ultimate ideal—the disappearance of the Jewish people.

Another aspect of the mechanics of dissolution makes clear a difficulty somewhat more subtle but even more effective. The death of a people or of a type can be natural only. Race suicide as an ideal is a contradiction, for an ideal is a manifestation of life. Deliberately to set before ourselves the objective of self-elimination would be as absurd

The Mechanism of Dissolution

as a man insisting on watching himself fall asleep. It can be done tacitly only. It can happen, but it cannot be propagated. We might drift out of consciousness, but every effort to accelerate the pace would retard the process. To appeal to Jews to cease to be Jews because they are Jews is to accentuate their Jewishness.

Of course the effort has been made, but with those grotesque and unnatural results which are in part responsible for your aversion to the process. There is nothing more ludicrous and pitiful than the Jew who has made his gentilization a deliberate ideal. His anxious self-repression, his self-disclaimers, his demand to be considered a gentile, his uneasy sense of inferiority, his impotent resentment of all that reminds him of his origin, make him an object of scorn alike to you and to us. There are "assimilated" Jews who hate with an ignoble and consuming hatred the "unassimilated" part of the Jewish people; Jews, who, rousing your secret contempt as renegades and your resentment as intruders, attribute their discomfort, falsely, to those Jews who are most obviously Jewish. For the gentilizing Jew is reluctant to admit that his very gentilization accentuates his Jewishness to you. His only recourse to save the last remnant of his self-respect is to blame the unassimilating Jew: in eager self-vindication he points at the object-lesson of the sufferings of orthodox and national Jewries and associates his own severer sufferings with the same cause. He deliberately ignores the fact that the cradle of the newer anti-Semitism is the country which witnessed the first efforts of the Jew to make a high ideal of assimilation. Germany, which in the nineteenth century offered the classic example of Jewish assimilation, both internal (in adaptation of our own life) and external (in baptism and inter-marriage) also became the country of classic anti-Semitism. Terrified at the infiltration of Jewish blood, the German gentile recast his formulæ of Jew-hatred in such wise as to arrest the process.

When we examine the mechanism of disso-

The Mechanism of Dissolution

lution in detail and come down to an examination of its working on the individual, we understand better the revolting character of at least its first effects. It is one thing to say that a people in the first stages of dissolution is as horrible a spectacle as a body in the first stages of putrefaction: but this sounds somewhat academic—perhaps even metaphysical. Even so there is little conveyed in the statement that a country is starving: we realize the import of the statement only when we speak of hungry men and women. When we examine the personal reactions of the deliberately assimilating Jew we see more clearly why he is not a pleasant spectacle either to Jew or to gentile.

A Jew who has made the repression of his Jewishness an ideal must be prepared to suffer and to seem to ignore every slight, every rebuff which he encounters. He must not permit an open sneer to sting him into Jewish self-consciousness: such a "weakness" would undo his purpose. He must seem to be unaware of the occasional coolness which follows the accidental revelation of his origin. He must bear silently with those countless unspoken snubs, half-snubs, unuttered queries, faint Ah-yes astonishments, which will be his lot until the day of his death. He must not feel himself implicated in a general slander of the Jews: he may only protest in a generous, disinterested sort of way, as a fair-minded "gentile." An angry retort or repudiation might be the ruin of him—he would suddenly realize the intolerable nature of his position. . . . It is not an easy thing to kill one's self by degrees.

Such a Jew has the whole way to go. He is not entering a world already made easier for him by an admixture of Jewish blood. He does not move forward to a partly prepared position. All is alien around him. His claims have no precedent. There is something pitifully impotent in his demand: "But I am an Englishman, like you; an American, like you. I have no affiliations outside of this country except those general human affiliations which I share with you. I feel for my

The Mechanism of Dissolution

co-religionists abroad nothing more nor less than you feel for your fellow-Christians among the Turks. Between me and my fellow-Jews in this country there is nothing more than between Protestant and Protestant, Catholic and Catholic." (Or, if he is baptized, this incriminating confession may presumably be omitted.) "I am part and parcel of your country. Our forefathers came later, but our posterity will stay as long. There is no difference between you and me except a very slight difference of faith—nothing really worth mentioning. In all else we are utterly alike. Do not let yourself be misled by the apparent contrast between me and my unassimilated co-religionists. It is merely a matter of externals. In a little while, in a generation or two, they will be like me—indistinguishable from you. They will be Americans (or Englishmen or Frenchmen) in every respect. Your destiny and ours, your outlook and ours, your hopes and ours, are identical."

But his plea falls on skeptical ears. There is that in the very name of Jew which invalidates his protestations. And the more vehemently he urges his case, the more suspicious and uneasy you become. For he is urging as an accomplished fact that which is nothing but a hopeless personal aspiration. Your demand is not connected with behavior or with views: neither of these makes the American or the Englishman. It is a question of identity. You want us to be Anglo-Saxons, or Teutons, if you are to call us Englishmen or Germans. And we cannot be that—at best our great-grandchildren can be as nearly that as matters. But *we* cannot remarry our great-grandparents.

We cannot but exasperate you by such importunate assumptions. That strangers, aliens to your blood, should come to dwell in your midst, is one thing. That they should claim, after a sojourn of a generation or two, complete identity with you, is as absurd as it is insolent. And even if they should dwell in your midst a thousand years, yet should keep apart, neither giving nor taking in marriage, they are not identical with you. In those

206

The Mechanism of Dissolution

words, "our ancestry," "our forefathers," there are implied the dearest and tenderest of human associations. The love of his forbears and of his posterity is all that man has of earthly immortality; the pride and affection which are the natural counterparts of these concepts are as narrow and as broad, as potent for good and evil, as sexual love, as life itself. Shall we come to you and share your *ancestry?* Shall we intrude on these exalted recollections, with a "we too"?

You cannot help resenting these claims. They savor at once of ingratiating humility and arrogant blasphemy. Try as you will you cannot make the concession. You are trapped by a vital paradox.

You may ask: What difference is there between a Jew claiming to be an American and an Italian claiming to be one? Is it more humiliating for one than for the other? Is the Italian of our ancestry more than you?

There is some similarity in the plight of all foreigners: and we Jews suffer all that foreigners suffer. But our case is unique because we are unique. If there is anything in what I have said, the cleft between you, Americans and Italians, Frenchmen and Germans, is but a wide jump as compared with the chasm between us and any one of you. What is true of the gentile foreigner in this regard is ten times true of us.

For our very record testifies against us. The older the past from which we attempt to flee, the closer it pursues us. To you, who share with us the human attribute of pride of ancestry, it seems incredible that, having retained our identity for a hundred generations, we should abandon it in one. It is suspicious —and odious. For you suspect (rightly) that in this tenacity of identity, which has outlived so many nations and civilizations, there is implied a kernel of individuality which is as singular in its nature as in its history.

Among yourselves assimilation is problem enough. The birth and death of nations is attended by wars, pains, humiliations. But what you have done a dozen times over in

208

the last four thousand years we have not done once.

We cannot assimilate: it is so humiliating to us that we become contemptible in submitting to the process: it is so exasperating to you that, even if we were willing to submit, it would avail us nothing.

XIV

Is There Any Hope?

THERE is little more to be said. I would only like to set down, before concluding, a few considerations which might help to clarify the issue between us. For I cannot believe that the contest between our two ways of life will come to an end within measurable time, and I cannot believe that while the contest continues it will ever be lifted to purely spiritual levels. I will not confound eschatology with daily experience: if ever the dream of the prophet should come true, if ever men should live at peace with each other, expressing their antagonisms without enmity—why, they will no longer be men, but another species, and talk of Jew and gentile will be as irrelevant then as it might have been twenty thousand years ago. The world is getting better, no doubt, but the improvement is not to be measured in generations or centuries, and what will come to pass ten thousand years from now does not concern me in connection with this problem. Certainly I have no patience with those who bid us wait dumbly for the apotheosis of mankind, as though the millennium were round the corner, as though every year registered a perceptible and even considerable improvement. If ever, within the span of one generation, mankind could suffer visible improvement, it should have been now, within the generation which witnessed the war. But only the fool and the professional optimist will assert that our way of life to-day, our utterances, our emotions, our ambitions, are at all cleaner than they were ten years ago, when the war started. The same handful of sensitive men and women struggle hopelessly against the passions of humanity: the same ugliness and meanness, the same selfishness and lying, the same lust for bloody adventure, the same delight in physical triumph, the same wilful self-deception and abuse of lovely phrases have us

211

in thrall. The race is still to the swift and the battle to the strong, and the goal and the prize are what they were ten years ago. What I say, then, is not prompted by the hope that words of mine—or of any one else—can give a new complexion to the general struggle between Jew and gentile: but only by the desire to clarify, for the encouragement of a few, the nature of this struggle, convincing them, perhaps, that behind the sordid stupidity which seems to govern our Jew-gentile relationship there may be found a compensating grain of eternal principle. And my concluding words are addressed less to practical expectations than to the desire for completeness.

What are we Jews prepared to give you which, in my opinion, you should consider sufficient? Obedience to the laws of the State and readiness to defend it (even if against our inmost belief) in time of danger. This constitutes a full payment for the privilege of citizenship and the protection of the laws.

But this offer on the part of the Jew be-

Is There Any Hope?

comes inadequate when the State begins to assume functions which seem to me totally beyond its capacity. What was intended only for the regulation of the external actions of a given group is becoming a growing tyranny against the inmost values of man, an attempted violation of our most inaccessible privileges. And this despite the professions of your statesmen and political thinkers.

It is acknowledged, in principle, that a man's religion is beyond the reach of law, and his God need neither pay taxes nor take out citizenship papers. But the acknowledgment of this principle is gradually becoming meaningless (perhaps it never had any meaning) in the light of the growing spiritual tyranny of the State. Perhaps nothing that you have ever feared from the economic tyranny of Socialism approaches the oppressive spiritual tyranny of your great democracies. These seek to control not only the acts, but the emotions of the individual. They would compel us to love and hate, to admire and despise, as part of our civic duty and, not content with that part of us which alone affects the well-being of government, would also conquer and control that part of us which belongs to no one but to each man and God.

They would control our culture, as though culture were controllable—except for the purpose of destruction—tell us in which language to create, as though they could fructify us, and direct our ecstasies, as though these were run along wires and commanded by switches. Our obedience, our tribute, our bodies, will not do: they would have the very secrets of the heart torn out of us and delivered to Washington or Berlin or London. In the terror of Socialism they depict the intolerable misery of the man who can claim nothing for himself, but must yield up the fruit of his labor, down to the last husk, to the disposition of the State. But they have instituted a spiritual Socialism infinitely more hideous, and for economic equality they have substituted a spiritual homogeneity which the communist can never hope to parallel in the physical field. And woe to him who dares to

214

practise private initiative in the spiritual-
Socialistic State! His punishment is not only
spiritual, but physical too. And we Jews, the
most obstinate and most enduring sinners in
this respect, are the best measure of the vin-
dictive fury with which this tyranny is armed.

If, then, the struggle between us is ever to
be lifted beyond the physical, your democracies will have to alter their demands for racial,
spiritual and cultural homogeneity within the
State. But it would be foolish to regard this
as a possibility, for the tendency of this civilization is in the opposite direction. There is
a steady approach toward the identification
of government with race, instead of with the
political State: and since this is largely beyond your conscious control, it is perhaps as
foolish as it is futile to expect a change. The
best fighting unit is a nation which is homogeneous in blood and emotions no less than
in political allegiance, and since the chief
function of the State is to fight (witness the
proportion of your taxes spent in payment
and in preparation for wars) you will inevi-

tably demand the subordination of all human functions to that end.

The demand for racial homogeneity within the State has led, in America—still the most unexploited country in the whole world —to the exclusion of the immigrant, and particularly of the immigrant who will not lend himself to the type of assimilation—or self-destruction—which you demand. Without for a moment admitting that any kind of exclusion is justifiable in a world which God created before the nations appeared to disfigure it, I submit the case of the Jew as an exception. The Jew has no homeland of his own. When the Jew migrates from one country to another, it is almost invariably under the pressure of persecution. To close the gate against the Jew is not the same, then, as closing it against the Italian or the Pole. In the latter cases you insist that certain races stay in their own homes—whether or not the land will support them. But the Jew is not being forced to stay at home: while one part of the gentile world persecutes him, the other part refuses him a chance to escape. For very shame—if you were capable of it— you should give the Jew free immigration everywhere. The irony of it is, of course, that it is chiefly against the Jew that anti-immigration laws are passed here in America as in England and Germany. And the liberal countries which could make room for the hunted Jew, coöperate, despite a few gallant and unsustained gestures, with the most illiberal in the persecution of their common victim. He that refuses asylum to a victim fleeing from a murderer is, before God, a free and willing accomplice in the crime.

And to me it is infinitely strange that, even from your point of view, the sporting point of view, you should be able to reconcile your morality with your acts. If there is anything at all in your professions, you should be filled with admiration and astonishment at the incredible pluckiness of a small people which, in the face of infinite discouragement, has clung with such tenacity to its identity and cult. Without understanding us at all, you

217

might have paid the homage of warriors to the courage of an unconquerable enemy.

That you watch us with vicious irritation rather than with respect, that you load us with contumely when so much in your own instinct should have given us a peculiar place in your regard, makes me feel that nothing which can be urged upon your conscience will avail to lighten the burden of our destiny. We have just witnessed, in America, the repetition, in the peculiar form adapted to this country, of the evil farce to which the experience of many centuries has not yet quite accustomed us. If America had any meaning at all, it lay in the peculiar attempt to rise above the trend of our present civilization—the identification of race with State. In the old world the evil had taken root in the course of centuries: its hideous fruit was therefore inevitable. But America seemed to offer the hope of a change: whatever other evils America had inherited, at least this one she had avoided. America was therefore the New World in this vital respect—that the State

Is There Any Hope?

wās purely an ideal, and nationality was identical only with acceptance of the ideal. But it seems now that the entire point of view was a mistaken one, that America was incapable of rising above her origins, and the semblance of an ideal-nationalism was only a stage in the proper development of the universal gentile spirit. The ideal which for a time constituted American nationality disappears now, and in its place emerges again, with atavistic certainty, the race.

It is true that even while the ideal flourished, triumphant over race, the seeds of our enmity lay securely imbedded in our natures. But the passing generosity kept the seeds in slumber. It is not the first time that gentile nations, forgetting themselves for a brief period, have offered us friendship and even affection. But the strange and unnatural exaltation passed, and bitter sobriety succeeded. To-day, with race triumphant over ideal, anti-Semitism uncovers its fangs, and to the heartless refusal of the most elementary human right, the right of asylum, is added cowardly insult. We are not only excluded, but we are told, in the unmistakable language of the immigration laws, that we are an "inferior" people. Without the moral courage to stand up squarely to its evil instincts, the country prepared itself, through its journalists, by a long draught of vilification of the Jew, and, when sufficiently inspired by the popular and "scientific" potions, committed the act.

How, then, shall I delude myself into the belief that the considerations covered in this chapter will produce any effect? Have we Jews not known this evil long enough? Should we not have known better, by this time, than to repose hope in any of the nations? Perhaps we were foolish in our overconfidence, but our credulousness does us less dishonor than your cruelty does you. And if it savors again of foolish simplicity to make this plea to you, I am willing to take the risk.

A LAST WORD

It would have been a happier task for me if I had been able to write this book, with sincerity, in another tone; if I had been able to record a struggle of two ideals and types which was never compromised and obscured by physical lusts and cruelties. But rather than utter the old, untruthful courtesies, tempering resentment with caution and tact, it would have been better not to write at all, and I was driven to write. I believe that though I may have erred here and there, I have been mainly right: and I console myself with the thought that if this book offends by its assertiveness, God knows that the infinite tactfulness of thousands of other Jews seems to have offended no less. Whatever we do we are damned—and I would rather be damned standing up than lying down.

Religion
75

CPSIA information can be obtained
at www.ICGtesting.com
Printed in the USA
LVHW040314190423
744769LV00008B/145